The Spiritual Legacy
of the American Indian

❖THE SPIRITUAL LEGACY OF THE AMERICAN INDIAN❖❖❖

Joseph Epes Brown

CROSSROAD · NEW YORK

1982

The Crossroad Publishing Company
575 Lexington Avenue
New York, New York 10022

Printed in the United States of America

Library of Congress Cataloging in Publication Data

Brown, Joseph Epes.
  The spiritual legacy of the American Indian.

  Includes bibliographical references.
  1. Indians of North America—Religion and
mythology. I. Title.
E98.R3B75 1982   299'.7   82-14924
ISBN 0-8245-0489-5

Grateful acknowledgment is made to the following for permission to reprint previ-
ously published material: The University of Oklahoma Press for excerpts from *The
Sacred Pipe* by Joseph Epes Brown, copyright 1953 by the University of Oklahoma
Press; the John G. Neihardt Trust for excerpts from *Black Elk Speaks* by John G.
Neihardt, copyright by John G. Neihardt, published by Simon & Schuster and the
University of Nebraska Press.

To *Hehaka* Sapa (Black Elk) who was a living representative
of the deepest spiritual wisdom of the Lakota people;
and to the distinguished Swedish scholar
Åke Hultkrantz
who has developed the special methodologies
by which American Indian religions are seen
in their full cultural and historical contexts

Contents

Acknowledgments

"The Spiritual Legacy" is reprinted by permission of Pendle Hill Publications from *The Spiritual Legacy of the American Indian* by Joseph Epes Brown, copyright © 1964 by Pendle Hill.

"The Roots of Renewal" appeared in *Seeing With A Native Eye*, edited by Walter Holden Capps. Copyright © 1976 by Walter Holden Capps. Reprinted by permission of Harper & Row, Publishers, Inc.

"The Persistence of Essential Values" was presented at the International Congress of the Istituto Accademico di Roma in 1968 and reprinted in *Conoscenga religiosa*, edited by Elémire Zolla.

"Contemplation Through Action" appeared in *Contemplation and Action in World Religions*, edited by Yusuf Ibish and Lleana Marculescu, copyright © 1977, 1978 by the Rothko Chapel and the De Menil Foundation.

"The Immediacy of Mythological Message" is reprinted with permission from Earle H. Waugh and K. Dad Prithipaul, editors, *Native Religious Traditions* (Waterloo, Ontario: Wilfrid University Press for the Canadian Corporation for Studies in Religion/Corporation Canadienne des Sciences Religieuses, 1979).

"Sun Dance: Sacrifice, Renewal, Identity" originally appeared in *Parabola*, vol. 3, no. 2 (Sacrifice and Transformation). Used with permission.

"The Question of 'Mysticism'" appeared in *Mystics and Scholars: The Calgary Conference on Mysticism, 1976*, edited by Harold Coward and Terence Penelhum, copyright © 1977 by the Canadian Corporation for Studies in Religion.

"Time and Process" is reprinted from *The Responsibility of the Academic Community in the Search for Absolute Values*, Proceedings of the Eighth International Conference on the Unity of the Sciences. (Los Angeles, 1979). By permission of the International Cultural Foundation Press. Copyright 1980 by the International Cultural Foundation, Inc.

"On Being Human" appeared in the booklet *The Religious Character of Native American Humanities: An Interdisciplinary Conference held April 14–16, 1977*, Department of Humanities and Religious Studies, Arizona State University, Tempe, Arizona.

Introduction

The chapters of this volume represent a selection of studies originally prepared for journals and conferences over at least the past decade. Due to the diversity of the publications and audiences, as well as the time span involved, it could well be asked what presiding or connective principles would give unity and cohesion to the total statement of this book. I can suggest two responses to this question, one historical and the other internal to the subject matter itself.

All of the chapter topics, which have been selected for the general reader, come out of a longstanding concern to develop the means by which selected and interrelated perspectives from the disciplines of cultural anthropology and the history of religions could be used to situate Native American spiritual heritages within the context of world religious traditions. This approach has made clear the necessity for reevaluating still existing Native American primal traditions, and in the process, to free them from outmoded prejudices that are revealed in such loaded polar terms as primitive and progressive, backward and developed, literate and illiterate, among others. All of the chapters of this book elaborate on this central concern by means of a wide range of specific examples drawn from selected Native American cultures.

A second factor contributing to the unity of this book is found in another different approach to the study and understanding of American Indian religions. It has now become abundantly clear that it is a fundamental and universal characteristic of Native American cultures, as indeed of all primal or primitive cultures, that "religion"—there is no equivalent word for this in any American Indian language—is not a separate category of activity or experience that is divorced from culture or society. Rather, religion is pervasively present and is in complex interrelationships with all aspects of the peoples' life-ways. The chapters of this book provide examples of the manner in which religious elements are integrated into, and give definition to, specific cultural expressions of the arts and crafts, music, subsistence activities, and social and political organizations. Necessarily each chapter focuses upon specific examples of this integration of religion, or the sacred, with daily life in the context of a particular tribal group.

In spite of the rich diversity of formal expressions in widely disparate cultures, all the chapters define a range of fundamental principles which is central to and operative within any one Native American culture. These shared principles underlie sacred concepts that are specific to each of nature's manifestations and also to what could be called sacred geography. There obtains, in addition, a special understanding of language in which words constitute distinct units of sacred power, just as in the visual arts the depicted form *is* what it represents. Such concepts of sacred forms extend to diverse architectural styles, so that each dwelling, no matter how simple, is an image of the cosmos. Dimensions of the sacred are made specific in every situation and are intensified through an enormous variety of special rites and ceremonies which embrace each person's life and the totality of *all* life. These fundamental principles, expressed in different cultural contexts through differing formal expressions, not only provide a thread of unity throughout the book, but collectively also represent a model of the multiple dimensions of the sacred which come together in an organic interrelated manner in any one Native American culture. I have attempted to arrange the chapters in a sequence that would progressively spell out and clarify these core sacred qualities.

The first introductory chapter attempts to outline and situate geographically diverse Native American cultures, languages, and religious traditions. It is evident that in the Americas generally, and in North America specifically, there is neither *an* American Indian tradition nor *a* spiritual legacy, but rather a rich variety of both. To ignore such diversity of origin, place, language, and resulting cultural forms, as is so often done under a plethora of stereotypes, is to do great disservice to the American Indian peoples and their history. Throughout this opening chapter particular emphasis is placed on the also forgotten reality that these are religious traditions which, for many if not most of the peoples concerned, are living realities. Indeed, the contemporary and presiding emphasis among the peoples is upon both the restoration or revitalization of traditions which may have become neglected or forgotten, and their taking educational systems into their own hands in order to meet their particular cultural needs.

The second chapter presents a sampling of religious themes drawn essentially from the Plains Indians. The third chapter emphasizes the contemporary mood for the renewal of traditional practices within the larger secular world. Chapter four documents with specific examples the amazing persistence of essential values within today's world of accelerating change. Chapter five documents a presiding and central theme of probably all Native American life-ways and religious traditions which stands in contrast to most Western religions and experience, since these tend to dichotomize, to emphasize, as in this case, an opposition between the domains of contemplation and action. By contrast, in the Native American world there generally obtains what may be called a unity in experience wherein actions of all orders serve as supports for contemplation, for the sacred is understood to be mysteriously present within all forms of the phenomenal world as well as within all modes of action. It is perhaps this most important non-dualistic mode of experiencing and being that is very difficult for the non-Indian Western mind to comprehend. Chapter six spells out in greater detail this general theme of unity in experience, but in this case emphasizes the immediacy of the message of myths, heightened through timing, staging, and the total dynamic process of mythic narration.

Chapter seven is a poetic statement about the Sun Dance that attempts to capture some of the dignity, beauty and profound heroic nature of this paramount ritual complex among the Plains Indians. The chapter following on mysticism stresses that among Native American peoples "mysticism" is not the vague "ism" as has so often become the case in certain Western contexts, but is rather a quality of spiritual participation which is framed and thus controlled by a range of specific rites involving the sacred forms of art, song, and dance. The rites and ceremonies of the Sun Dance itself, or the ritualized supports and requirements of the vision quest, are examples of frameworks through which sacred experiences are received and given direction in the life of the recipient. Chapter nine outlines the implications of the dominant contemporary concepts of linear and segmented time as contrasted with the rhythmical and cyclical concepts of time that are universally held in the original traditions of Native American peoples. The concluding chapter summarizes many of the values presented in preceding chapters, but with emphasis here upon the spiritual quality of the person which participation in such values and realities tend to form.

"We are all related" is a statement of profound implication made by each Lakota after he or she has smoked a sacred pipe in common and in communion. It is hoped that something of this quality of relationship is sensed throughout this book.

JOSEPH EPES BROWN

The Spiritual Legacy
of the American Indian

North American Indian Living Religions

The following treatment of elements of American Indian living religions must be both cursory and selective. Even where emphasis is to be upon the present living reality and viability of religious elements, account must be taken of at least the following three major interrelated factors.

First, American Indian religions represent preeminent examples of primal religious traditions that have been present in the Americas for some thirty to sixty thousand years. Fundamental elements common to the primal nature of those traditions not only survive into the present among Indian cultures of the Americas, but in many cases are currently being reexamined and reaffirmed by the people with increasing and remarkable vigor.

Second, out of this heritage of primal qualities there has developed, through time and in accord with the great geographical diversity of the Americas, a rich plurality of highly differentiated types of religious traditions, making it impossible to define or describe American Indian religions in generalities.

Third, ever-increasing contacts since the late fifteenth century with representatives of diverse civilizations and cultures of Europe and Euro-Americans led to a vast spectrum of change within and across indigenous Indian cultures. Under this impact certain tribal groups and even linguistic families became extinct, while others became acculturated to varying degrees into the dominant societies.

Most surviving groups, however, have shown through history a remarkable ability for coping with change and cultural deprivation by adapting and borrowing from the non-Indian world with pragmatic yet cautious selectivity, making it possible not just to survive but to retain at least core elements of ancient and well-tried religions and traditional ways of being. The "new" religious movements of revitalization or reformulation, in response to deprivation and continuing pressures for acculturation, should therefore be understood in terms of a continuity of traditional elements rather than as innovations unrelated to the peoples' own religious and cultural history. The impact of Christianity and the special meaning of "conversion" to the American Indian should also be understood in this larger context.

THE PRIMAL FOUNDATIONS

Those primal elements that are universal and fundamental to virtually all North American Indian religious traditions of past or present include the following general qualities or traits.

1. That which we refer to in current usage as "religion" cannot be conceived as being separable from any of the multiple aspects of any American Indian culture. In no American Indian language is there any single word or term that could translate as "religion," as there is no single term for what we refer to as "art." To stress this distinctive phenomenon it is preferable to use a term such as "traditions," or perhaps, for greater clarity, "religious traditions," when referring to religion among American Indians or indeed among any primal peoples.

types, a thousand or more tribal groups with several hundred mutually unintelligible languages for North America alone, and all with the contrasts of American geography and climatic zones to which the peoples adapted, present complexities and questions that still evade scholars. Full descriptions and formulations of typologies within the subtle and sensitive area of native religious traditions is a work still to be accomplished, and is further complicated by historical overlays of Euro-American presences and their introduction, with proselytizing zeal and quasi-divine mandate, of new religiocultural elements. The appended map of "culture areas" (p. 131) will express and perhaps clarify some elements of this grand complexity.

In response to increasing evidence of this cultural plurality, the concept of Native American "culture areas" was conceived and developed at the turn of the century by Clark Wissler. This is a concept that necessarily oversimplifies and raises problems, such as its static perspective and the cultural identity of people where areas converge and overlap. Yet the device is deemed useful here as a means for organizing descriptive materials and for employing certain generalizations within circumscribed limits. The five culture areas that have been selected for summary description both represent a cross-section of North American indigenous peoples and provide examples of religious traditions as related to contrasting subsistence patterns.

The general primal qualities already outlined, with the more specific traits to be described, may be said to constitute *living* religions in the sense that core elements of sacred lore, values, and the native language are held and lived today by at least certain segments of the populations, and it is through the leaders of these groups that movements for preservation and revitalization are appearing with increasing frequency. Analysis of the impact and meaning of Christianity and conversion among American Indian groups will be presented in the concluding part of this chapter.

THE ARCTIC ESKIMO

The Eskimo of the arctic coast, whose religious traits are representative of a larger circumpolar region, are often excluded from descriptions of the more southern Indians. Such exclusion is arbitrary, since evidence suggests that many core arctic and closely related subarctic religious themes diffused southward, where, with certain modifications and additions, they survive today in the lives of eastern woodland Algonquin hunting peoples, among the Athabascans of the western subarctic, and even among the peoples of the Plains and Prairie cultural area.

The Eskimo experience their world of barren coast and expanse of sea and ice as peopled with a vast host of spirit beings whose differentiated qualities and associated powers are specific to each form and force of the natural environment. There are also spirits, no less real, which are of realms unrelated to forms of the phenomenal world. Graphic depiction of such spirit realities is expressed by the people in abundance, as executed in the ancient tradition of stone carvings or through contemporary innovative lithographs, as produced, for example, by the peoples of the Cape Dorset Cooperatives. Precarious subsistence dependency upon sea mammals, or land animals in season, is interrelated with beliefs in a soul or plurality of souls specific to all human and nonhuman living beings. In slaying animals of the sea or land, the hunter thus bears grave responsibility for releasing souls (*anua*) of living beings; rites and ceremonies must therefore be observed in relation to all aspects of hunting. The Eskimo indeed hold that the greatest danger in their lives is not the cold or constant threat of starvation, but the presiding reality that their existence is dependent upon the taking of life from other beings. In a world where such precarious balance obtains between life and death, or where such a thin line divides physical appearances from the subtle realm of spirits, it is understandable that there must be specific structures and mechanisms by which equilibrium can be maintained.

Equilibrium within families and larger social groups depends upon observing a host of taboos specific to every necessary activity and social interrelationship. Where codes of such appropriate behavior are broken, or where the attitudes of the hunter are not respectful toward the game, it is believed that the animals will not present themselves willingly as a sacrificial offering to the hunter.

These traditions of the coastal arctic peoples are expressed and supported by beliefs in an all-powerful goddess, half human and half fish, called Sedna or Takanaluk, who dwells in a great cave or pool under the sea wherein she keeps all the sea mammals, which she will release or withhold according to the degree to which the people observe or break the taboos. In parallel manner, there are Masters or Keepers of the various species of land animals, who will release or withhold their kind according to the behavior and attitudes of the hunter and the hunter's people. These beliefs suggest the presence of an abstract and unifying concept, since the multiplicity of spirits and souls of all sea life coalesce into a kind of unity in the single underwater Sea Power, as in similar manner the spirits of land animals are unified under the single great Master or Keeper. Although it is not possible to affirm for the Eskimo an even more ultimate concept of a High God responsible for all life, as is found in most Indian tribes to the south, there nevertheless is occasional reference to a unity of all living beings of sea and land in the figure of the Great Meat Dish. If such seemingly more ultimate and unitary concept may not be central to Eskimo experience, it could well be due to the fact that human survival here necessitates presiding attention to the immediate and specific elements of a harsh and precarious environment.

In this arctic world of uncertainties, the central and all-important religious practitioner is the *angákut,* or shaman,

which is the customary Siberian Tungusic term. This shaman helps the people maintain the necessary delicate balance between this world of pragmatic necessities and the
more subtle, but no less real world of spirits, souls, and
gradated powers. The shaman is an intermediary between
these multiple worlds, who can communicate, interpret,
and indeed travel in mysterious flight through the worlds of
Eskimo realities. The shaman's wisdom and special powers
are critical to communal life and human survival. Through
the shaman's familiarity with the spirit realms and through
his ability to send out in ecstatic trance one of his souls,
often called the "free soul," on a spiritual journey and
quest, he is able to discern who among the people has broken the taboos causing the disappearance of the game. He is
able to placate Sedna under the sea, or discover the cause of
illness perhaps associated with "soul loss," or he may fore-
tell future weather conditions and thus the appropriate time
for travel.

Methods of becoming a shaman are common to many Indian groups of the Americas. The apprentice must have a
guide who has traveled and knows the way. Among many
disciplines, he must learn from his instructor how to divest
himself, in sacred and mysterious manner, of the outer lay-
ers of his own flesh, and then to name all the bones of his
skeleton. In such magical lore is clarified the deep meanings underlying widespread traditions of shamanic art forms
found throughout the arctic and Indian Americas, wherein
the outer covering of beings is understood and presented as
transparent, a kind of x-ray vision that focuses on depicted
inner or vital realities understood in a spiritual manner. To
gain the shamanic lore, the apprentice must also participate
in a retreat where, through the secrets of solitude and in
suffering through fasting and exposure to cold, he will receive, if he is worthy, specific sacred powers through the
vision appearance and the teachings of a helping spirit.

The novice shaman must then observe special taboos and
requirements when he returns to his people, whom he is

now able to lead through the delicate balance of life and death as an intermediary for the subtle forces of the spirit worlds. Demonstration of the powers received is required in periodic communal gatherings where, with the aid of the powerful rhythms of drum and voice, and with a rich array of dramatic props and techniques, the shaman enters into ecstatic trance, during which his soul travels to find and return with the needed knowledge. His success or failure as a shaman is established for the people in accord with the pragmatic or spiritual results obtained. Such practices and shamanic lore confirm for the people the realities of the worlds of spirits and souls, afford release from personal and communal tensions, and define order and structures critical to stability and continuity of the family and larger society in a harsh and precarious environment.

THE EASTERN SUBARCTIC

Religious elements central to the arctic peoples are reca-pitulated, with certain variations and additions, in the lives of the northern Algonquin hunters who adapted to condi-tions of the boreal regions of the subarctic. In spite of changes wrought by a long history of contact with Euro-American hunters, trappers, traders, and Christian mission-aries, the hunting activities of these people are still imbued with sacred beliefs and accompanying rites similar in most respects to those of the arctic. Here, however, are found rich mythologies of creation with an anthropomorphic Creator fig-ure who is found upon the primordial waters, accompanied by already present aquatic diving birds and animals, and who brings to the surface of the waters the primal mud from which the earth is fashioned. This mythic theme instructs, among many other things, that creation is not just an event of time past but is an ever-continuing process in which all elements of creation participate now as always.

Also, there are tales of ambivalent Trickster hero figures

who bring desirable things to the people while defining through their unacceptable acts the parameters of acceptable behavior. The conical-frame wigwam type of dwelling is conceived by the people as a recreated image of the cosmos, or of the human being as a microcosm, as is also reflected in the dome-shaped "sweat lodge." In such lodges the regenerative forces of earth, air, fire, and water are used in combination for restoring a man's original purity, which may be lost through the breaking of innumerable hunting taboos or through contact with the ritual impurity associated with the menstrual cycles of women. The smoking pipes and tobacco used in this area carry eminently sacred and sacramental meanings. Although it is true that tobacco smoking is found on the arctic coast, evidence suggests that its origin is from the west, from Russia through Siberia, which explains the absence of sacred elements associated with smoking among the Eskimo.

The religious practitioners of the western and eastern subarctic represent a modification of the classic shamanism of the arctic and Siberia, for here the shaman does not send out in ecstatic trance one of his souls to accomplish a mission; rather, in dramatic ceremony within the lodge, and with the use of the drum and offerings, he conjures *in* to himself his spirit helpers, whom he had experienced in the course of a vision quest. These spirits demonstrate their presence by mysteriously tapping and shaking the lodge, at times accompanied by mysterious sounds. The spirits, who are sometimes the practitioner's guardian spirits, are then instructed to seek out and bring back what is desired of them.

As is appropriate to a people whose lives are dependent upon the hunting and trapping of large and small game, there obtains rich and sacred lore relating to all the animals in their world of experience. Special qualities are specific to each species of animal, and these qualities can be communicated to the people. Animals are thus considered as teachers and, in a sense, are therefore superior to humans. Due to such beliefs the people have secret societies of animal lodges, which often are ranked in accordance with the powers specific to the particular animal. The bear, for example, is considered to be of the greatest power, thus complex rites and ceremonies are found in the hunting, slaying, and final sacramental treatment of this animal, especially concerning the appropriate and respectful disposal of the bones and skull. The key Algonquin term that refers to sacred power as used here is *manitu*, with *Kitchi Manitou* being the totality of all such powers. It is suggested by certain scholars that the latter term, which suggests an overall unitary principle, originated with the coming of Christianity; yet it is also highly probable, as much evidence suggests, that this concept was understood prior to the advent of Euro-Americans.

EASTERN WOODLANDS

Moving southward from the coastal arctic to the subarctic and into the eastern woodlands, there is a cumulative continuity of core religious themes, their ritual and ceremonial expressions increasingly complex as climate and habitat become more favorable. Such complexity is well illustrated by the Medewewin medicine dance, or the Medicine Lodge Society of the Ojibwa-Chippewa of the Great Lakes region. These ceremonies normally occur semiannually in late spring and early fall. Candidates seek initiation into the sacred society for a variety of reasons, but most often they have had dream or vision experiences in retreats that indicate they should seek admission. Such persons are then instructed by the *mide* priests in the sacred lore, songs, and other requirements for entry.

The Medewewin rites are conducted within a long lodge conceived as an image of the universe. Purification in a sweat lodge is required prior to participation in the ceremonies. Within the lodge, and guarding the doorways, are cer-

tain forms identified with animal-spirit helpers and guard-
ians. The rites may last from two to eight days, depending
on the degrees the candidates are entering. The first of these
cumulative degrees is associated with aquatic animals referred to in myths of creation: the mink, otter, muskrat, or
beaver. The second degree is associated with the beings of
the air, an owl or a hawk, and the third degree with more
powerful beings of the earth such as the serpent or wildcat.
The fourth and ultimate degree, which may be achieved in
older age and which demands much time, preparation, and
expense, is represented by the most powerful land animal,
the bear. Within the lodge myths are recited by the priests
or medicine men that tell of creation and sacred migration,
such recitations usually supported by incised birch-bark
scrolls, which act as a mnemonic acid. The ceremonies
come to a dramatic climax when the candidates are ritually
"shot" by the priests, using an otterskin bag out of which the
sacred *mi'gis* or cowrie shell is magically propelled into the
candidate, who drops to the ground experiencing a spiritual
death. In being brought back to life by the priest, the candidate is understood to be reborn into a new world of deeper
spiritual understanding.

Although these Algonquin peoples have had intense contacts over many centuries with Euro-American peoples and
cultures, and have experienced loss of lands, new types of
subsistence economies, the introduction of Christianity, and
most recently the new syncretistic Peyote religion of the
Native American Church, rites such as those of the Medewewin are not only still observed, but there is evidence of
increasing participation. Such renewed affirmation of traditional religious elements may in part be explained by the
new pan-Indian movements, which so facilitate intertribal
exchange that other centers of traditional renewal, as found
for example in the Plains, provide example and stimulus to
tribal groups of distant areas.

The dominant Iroquoian-speaking peoples of a still more

favorable eastern woodland environment represent even greater cultural complexity in their dual subsistence patterns of horticulture, probably of southeastern origin, and seasonal hunting. Their wise and well-known sociopolitical league organization of the six nations, although somewhat changed and modified, is still intact and operative today in its basic structure, as is the case with many of the traditional Iroquoian religious expressions that endure beneath the obvious external evidence of change.

Iroquoian religion gives ultimate attention to a supreme and unitary principle which, although claimed by many to be of Christian origin, nevertheless seems to be integral from the earliest times to a host of core indigenous Iroquoian expressions and general world view. Their term *Orenda*, which defines an extension of spiritual power(s), is a concept which, although expressed in different languages, is widespread across American Indian cultures. Such an abstract concept is basic to Iroquoian cosmologies, which define dualisms of heaven and earth, but which understand them to be necessary reciprocal forces that are ultimately inherent in a unitary principle. The structure of the Iroquoian longhouses expresses these cosmological values, and it is in such houses that the people to this day enact cycles of complex four-day dance-drama ceremonies, often of thanksgiving, acknowledging and celebrating the gifts of life in the form of foods both wild and cultivated.

The Iroquoian carved masks of the False Face curing societies speak of the spirit forces of the woodlands, their powers intensified by the requirement that the marks be carved out of a standing living tree. The Iroquois have rites of purification, and youths are expected at puberty to engage in the vision quest, often to seek out a personal guardian spirit, which is usually associated with the person's new and sacred name. With the disruption of much of Iroquoian culture under an intensity of Euro-American contact and pressures for change, there appeared in the 1800s the Seneca prophet Handsome Lake, whom the people prefer to call the Life Bringer, who brought a messianic message with strict codes of conduct. As with the messianic movement of the 1890 Ghost Dance, or the Peyote cult that became incorporated as the Native American Church in 1918, the code of the Iroquois Life Bringer integrated traditional indigenous elements with selected Christian ethics and beliefs. It is in terms of such synthetic reformulations that members of the Iroquois league live their religions today.

The Plains and Prairie

Native American groups living today in the Plains and Prairie area represent very diverse cultural histories, with tribal origins tracing back to the hunting cultures of the Athabascan Mackenzie subarctic, the eastern Algonquin woodlands, and the early agricultural traditions of the Southeast, as well as to certain groups of Uto-Aztecan gathering and hunting peoples from the Great Basin area. Given this great diversity of origins, languages, and cultures, it is difficult to understand in what sense this geographic zone may be said to constitute a single culture area with distinctive religious traditions. Yet over many centuries, with common adjustments to a unique Plains and Prairie grasslands environment supporting millions of bison, and with the advent of the horse in the 1800s leading to greater mobility and intensification of intertribal contacts, the diverse groups developed a style of life and thought expressing a commonality of religiocultural traits. This cultural history presents a remarkable example of adaptability and selective borrowings that has continued into the present day even in confrontations with new elements and forces for change from Euro-American societies. It is this facility for adaptation that has allowed the people to survive with a distinctive Plains style and quality of core religious and ceremonial elements.

The Plains people define and experience a multitude of differentiated spirit beings or sacred powers, which (a) are specific to each form and element of the natural world; (b) are associated with vital force or an animating life principle; and (c) possess subtle qualities understood to be transferable to other beings or even to "inanimate" forms. It should be noted that in the people's experience no hard dichotomy obtains between the Western categories of "animate" and "inanimate," since to them all phenomena are animate in some manner. The sacred quality of powers is denoted by terms such as the Dakota *Wakan,* which is not a noun with the implication of limit, but an adjective conveying a sense of mystery or the mysterious. This multiplicity of sacred mysteries tends to coalesce into an ultimate unity expressed through polysynthetic terms such as the Lakota *Wakan-Tanka,* "Great Mysterious," similar to *Wakonda* among the Omaha and Osage. The often-used translation "Great Spirit" employs a noun, and is undoubtedly the result of a Christian perspective that changes the original sense of the term.

Almost all Plains tribal groups stress the importance of individual participation in a ritualized "vision quest," or less frequently a quest to receive one's personal guardian spirit, both forms being accomplished in solitary retreat with fasting and sacrifice. Sacred powers appearing in such experiences are usually associated with animal beings or with other natural phenomena, and they may indicate the seeker's sacred name, may constitute the origin and validation of sacred songs and forms of art, or may be the origin of a new tribal rite or ceremony. The nature of the received vision often obligates the recipient to externalize the experience and thus to share the power with the larger community through use of art representations or an actual reenactment of the experience through new forms of dance-drama. The obligation for all individuals to participate in a vision quest is so pervasive that Robert Lowie was led to term the trait "democratized shamanism."

The classical dwelling of Plains peoples is the portable conical tipi, which expresses cosmological and metaphysical meanings and is therefore still used for ceremonial occasions or for general communal gatherings such as the summer "powwows." The shelter is understood as the universe, or microcosmically as a human person. The central open fire is the presence of the Great Mysterious, which is at the center of all existence, and the smoke hole at the top of the tipi is the place and path of liberation. Similar understandings are specific to the small dome-shaped sweat lodge wherein, as with the eastern subarctic peoples, purification rites are required as preparation for sacred ceremonies, or before any important undertaking. Even though today most Plains people live in permanent frame houses, the purification lodges are usually found nearby.

The Sun Dance, also called Medicine Dance or Thirst Lodge, is an annual springtime world- or self-renewal ceremony of great complexity, which today has been particularly instrumental in the preservation and revitalization of many traditional religious elements. The large, circular open frame lodge is ritually constructed in imitation of the world's creation, with the sacred cottonwood tree at the center as the axis linking sky and earth. Those who have previously made the vow participate in the sacrificial dance-fast in the lodge for three to four days, dancing all day and most of the night with the powerful support of large drums and heroic songs. They move from the circumference to the tree at the center and back again, always facing and concentrating upon the tree at the center, or upon one of the sacred objects attached to the tree—an eagle or bison head or skull. Some groups, such as the Lakota, periodically move within the lodge in such a manner that the dancers are always gazing toward the sun, which is associated with the source of life. Some dancers make specific vows to pierce the muscles of their chests. Into these cuts are attached thongs that have been tied to a high point in the tree, so that the dancer is now virtually tied to the center and must dance until the flesh breaks loose. Through the rigors and sacrificial elements of these rites the individual participants often receive powers through vision experiences, and the larger community gathered in support of the dancers participates in the sacred powers thus generated.

The sacred tobacco pipes of the Plains peoples express in comprehensive synthetic manner all that is most sacred to the people. Such pipes are used on all ritual and important occasions, and any agreement or relationship sealed with the smoking of a pipe is held inviolate. Such pipes have sacred origins defined in rich mythologies, and there are pervasive beliefs, held to this day, that if ever the pipes are no longer used or respected the people will lose their center and will cease to be a people. The pipes, which have long wooden stems and stone bowls, are understood to be an axis joining and defining a path between heaven and earth. Microcosmically the pipe is identified with human beings, the stem being the breath passage leading to the bowl, which is the spiritual center or heart. In solemn prayer, as each grain of carefully prepared tobacco is placed in the pipe, mention is made of some aspect of creation, so that when the bowl is full it contains the totality of time, space, and all of creation including humankind. When the fire consumes this consecrated tobacco with the aid of human breath, there is affirmed the absorption, or identity, of all creation with the fire, which is the presence of the ultimate Great Mysterious. Often, in concluding the rite the participants in the communal smoking recite, "We are all related." Today certain Christian priests, realizing the profound meanings of the pipe, are attempting to integrate the rites within the context of celebration of Holy Communion. On the other hand, many of the younger traditional Indians have ambivalent feelings about such practices.

Religious practitioners in the Plains are often termed "medicine men" or "medicine women," for they are the ones who know the lore of curative herbs, a knowledge partly transferred but validated and added to through sacred lore received in the vision quest. There are also those who have received especially sacred powers and helpers through vision or dream experiences and are thereby qualified to guide others in the means to seek experience of the sacred. Both functions are often possessed by one person.

This type of person and function is somewhat different from the classical arctic shaman, for here the practitioner does not send out his or her "free soul" in a trance state to accomplish missions, but rather in dramatic ceremony the spirit helpers are called in and then sent out to discover the cause of illness, to find lost objects, or to provide an answer to some spiritual question. The contemporary Yuwipi ceremonies, now very popular among the Sioux, provide good examples of such a type of practitioner and the use of what may be called ceremonial magic.

Purification rites, vision quests, Sun Dances, rituals of the pipe, and other ceremonies of a traditional nature are being increasingly practiced by Plains peoples today, with positions of leadership being assumed by younger tribal members. Affirmation of certain traditional values is also being expressed in new contexts and through such means as the summer "powwow" circuit, offering a type of nomadism with intertribal pan-Indian emphasis. Even the once militant American Indian Movement, which used religious themes to support protest activities, is now minimizing militant protest in favor of sincere relearning and reliving the traditional religious ways in which more ultimate and lasting answers to problems and questions of identity are found. Statistics are not available, but significant evidence from Plains areas strongly suggests that the once rapidly expanding ceremonial use of peyote in the syncretistic Native American Church is now being superseded by the more satisfying and lasting realities found in the roots of the people's own indigenous traditional lore, which, moreover, is carried by their own languages.

THE SOUTHWEST

Due to rich cultural and linguistic diversity the American Southwest as a cultural area is so complex that it is only possible to treat here in summary manner two dominant groups, the Pueblos and Navajo, or *Dinwe* (the people), as they prefer to be called.

The roots of the sedentary Pueblo cultures in the Southwest reach back to both the Paleo-Indian big game hunters of approximately 10,000 B.C. and to the expansive Desert Culture of ±3000 B.C. with its evidence of incipient agriculture. Since these ancient times, the peoples have developed rich and complex cultures identified with specific regions and experienced a number of migrations before being located at their present sites along the Rio Grande in the east and extending to the Arizona mesas of the Hopi in the west.

The very distinct Athabascan (*Na Diné*)-speaking Navajo appeared in the Southwest as recently as A.D. 1200–1400, having migrated south from their homelands in the Yukon-Mackenzie subarctic area. In the interrelationships between the Navajo and Pueblo peoples, and in the encounter of both groups with the later Spanish and Euro-American domination, they have each been able to retain into the present day their own unique identities. Remarkable examples are here found not only of cultural persistence throughout adaptation and change, but also of the enduring viability of the Navajo, whose original population in 1868 was approximately eight thousand; fifty thousand in 1950; eighty-five thousand in 1961; and at least one hundred and seventy-five thousand at present.

The Pueblos

It could be assumed that the Pueblos, as sedentary agricultural village people, would be especially vulnerable to those successive outside pressures for change on the part of the Spanish explorers and military, the Christian missionaries, and the detraditionalizing policies of the American government agencies. And yet through time and bitter experience the communities learned the wisdom of appearing to acquiesce while holding in secret to their own traditional beliefs and sacred rites and ceremonies. The profound and all-encompassing nature of these traditions, borne by languages the oppressors did not understand, explains the remarkable continuity and viability of the Pueblo peoples into the present day.

Although each of the many Pueblo communities holds to its own distinctive ways of belief and action, it is nevertheless possible to suggest certain generalizations if the differences are understood to be dialects of a commonly shared cosmological and spiritual language. The Pueblo cosmos is defined through mythic narrations expressing a varying number of spheres pierced through by a hollow vertical axis. Among the Zuni these spheres are described as seven in number. Commencing with the realm of A'wonawil'ona, understood as a supreme life-giving bisexual power, other spheres are identified in turn with the Sun Father, who gives light and warmth, and the Moon Mother, who gives light at night, divides the year into months, and expresses the life cycle of living beings. The central terrestrial fourth realm is of the Earth Mother, the provider of all vegetation. The fifth subterrestrial realm is associated with the gods of war, the twin culture heroes, and the sacred Corn Mother. The gods of the sixth realm are represented by persons wearing masks (the *koko*), who appear in the seasonal dance-drama, and the seventh realm is identified with the zoic gods.

Mythic accounts of the coming into being of human persons and animals in the terrestrial realm commence with descriptions of a dark underworld, an eminently sacred realm of undeveloped possibility. In the process of emerging into the terrestrial realm, amorphous "human" beings are led by solar heroes and are also aided by animal beings who explore in turn each sphere to the four horizontal cardinal directions. The actual process of vertical emergence is aided by four types of sacred trees identified with each of the four directions and upon which the beings climb upward to emerge into this world of limit and hardness but illuminated by the light of the sun.

It is through the full context of these myths, periodically retold in dramatic manner, that everything of importance for the people of this present terrestrial realm is defined: the heavenly elements of sun and moon, the four directions of horizontal space with their specific colors and identifying mountain ranges, the meanings associated with categories of trees, and the rich lore specific to each of the animals and birds, which is central to the structure and values of the people's many secret societies.

The Pueblo cosmos may be defined in terms of the duality of sacred worlds below in distinction to the more profane world into which the peoples emerged—comparatively a realm of hardness, limit, and restricted possibility. Among the Tewa peoples this dualism is defined through terms such as *ochu* (green, unripe, eminently sacred) in distinction to *seht'a* (cooked, ripe, or hardened); social categories, with their supernatural or posthumous counterparts, are defined and supported by such formulations. Thus it is clear why the most sacred places within the Pueblos are the *kivas*, or underground ceremonial chambers, at the bottom of which is a hollow shaft, the *sipapu*, leading underground and understood to be the very place of emergence, the Center of centers, and the underworld connection to the shrines located in the sacred mountains of the four directions. Within these kivas, present in varying numbers within each Pueblo, preparations take place for ceremonial rites and the dance-dramas of the masked deities that are enacted in accord with a carefully observed ceremonial calendar based on the seasons marked by the dualities of summer and winter solstices. The strict observance of the ceremonial cycle is controlled by a priest of a specific clan, who observes the annual movements of the sun. Access to the underground kiva is through a vertical ladder, so that descent and ascent recapitulates for the person the mythic process of emergence; it is also the way of access back to the sacred realm. The dance-dramas, which are prepared by the men in the kivas, are enacted in the appropriate season in the open village plazas; this periodic return of the deities reestablishes contact with the realm of the sacred.

Without the seasonal enactment of these rites and ceremonies it is believed that recycling of the sacred world- and life-sustaining powers will cease, the world will die, and the people will be no more. The pervasive force of such ritually enacted beliefs inhibits acculturation into the non-Pueblo world of other and predominantly secular values. The comprehensive nature of beliefs integrated into the totality of lifeways makes unattractive and unnecessary the taking on of new religious elements or movements from the non-Pueblo outside world. The Native American Church and the multiple Christian denominations have therefore made little inroad into Pueblo life.

The Navajo

As northern intruders into a southwestern area of enormous cultural complexity, it is understandable that many threads of present-day Navajo culture represent a complex of elements borrowed from the Pueblos, the Spanish, the Spanish-Americans, and the ever-changing presence of the American non-Indian world. The impact of these influences is intensified by the structured presence of increasing numbers of Christian missions of all denominations, by the endless stream of "civilizing" educational policies and various agents of the U. S. government, and by new religious movements such as the Native American Church. Yet in spite of obvious changes within ancient Athabascan lifeways resulting from these contacts and pressures, studies such as that of Evan Vogt[1] suggest that these multiple innovative elements, with the exception of certain Pueblo traits, have not become fused in an integrative manner into Navajo culture and world view or compartmentalized—as was the Pueblo response to pressures for change—but have been sequentially *incorporated* around a central structural framework that was and remains to this day distinctly Navajo. The essence of this persistent structure is identified with elements of a basic Athabascan heritage of material and nonmaterial elements reinterpreted through creative adaptations drawn from Pueblo cosmologies and ceremonial expressions.

Central to the Navajo view of the world and reality is the understanding that the human personality is a whole with every facet interrelated both within itself and in relationship to the totality of phenomena seen and unseen. Within this interrelated totality everything exists in two parts, the good and bad, the positive and negative, or the elements of male and female; they complement each other and belong together. Normally these elements are balanced, harmonious, ordered, and thus beautiful. This ideal equilibrium, however, is precarious and may be put out of balance through an indefinite number of possible factors that must be avoided; doing anything to excess, the violation of taboos, contamination through contact with the ghosts of the dead, harboring evil thoughts, initiating or being the victim of acts of witchcraft, or any disrespect or carelessness in one's relationships with the forms and forces of a natural world that normally is in a state of balance and harmony.

Symptoms of any illness whatsoever are indications that the normal balance and harmony has been upset, and therefore must be restored. Such restoration of health for the Navajo person necessitates participation in one of several hundred ceremonial "chantways" of from two to nine or even fourteen days' duration. The chantway specific to the illness is determined by a special quasi-shaman diagnostician or "hand trembler." A singer (*hatali*) who knows the particular selected chantway is then contacted, and elaborate preparations are commenced. Sacred ceremonies must always be enacted within a *hogan,* the traditional Navajo circular or octagonal dwelling with an opening in the domed roof. Such dwellings, as well as the Athabascan-type conical sweat lodge, are considered by the people to be the world or cosmos, with its place of release in the opening above. Reminiscent of the Pueblos is the use of plumed prayer wands, which are set in the four directions outside the ceremonial hogan as a means to compel the *Yei* (gods) to come and be present with their curative spiritual powers. Central to the long and complex ceremonies within the hogan is the chanting by the singer of myths of creation, the episodes of heroes who purified the earth in primal times, or of other sacred mythic episodes that have specific relationship to the primary cause of the illness in question. These chants must be recited without any error of commission or omission whatsoever. At appropriate times, multicolored sandpaintings are laid out with great precision on the clean sand of the hogan floor, upon the center of which the patient is seated so that the curative powers of the depicted gods, and of other beings and forms of power, may work for the restoration of harmony, balance, and thus health. Although the patient is the central beneficiary of these sacred rites, it is understood that powers thus generated spread out from the center to bless others who are present and eventually extend outward without limit.

Because the presiding ideal of their religious tradition is the maintenance of balance and harmony in interrelationships with the total environment, it is understandable that the Navajo are under considerable internal stress and tension in their confrontations with a surrounding world that is dominating, threatening, and unpredictable. Participation with this larger American world in foreign wars has intensified these pressures, even though the Navajo are very proud of their abilities in warfare, for slaying an enemy involves contact with the potentially dangerous ghost of the dead.

One avenue of controlled release from such tensions has long been the intensification on the reservation of witchcraft practices. Because such practices are institutionalized, they do not jeopardize the basic structures and foundations of Navajo life. Other types of possibly more positive responses are in a sense paradoxical, for they have resulted, on the one hand, in intensification of traditional ceremonial activities in order to "decontaminate" those who have been exposed to dangerous forces associated with either the dead or the unfamiliar. On the other hand, and with the pragmatic sense that the Navajo have always shown, they now seek any available additional means for curing their ever-increasing and complex ailments. Here is found at least partial explanation for the Navajo's willing utilization of non-Indian health services, or for their increasing participation in the Native American Church, wherein their central focus is upon the use of the hallucinogenic peyote as curative agent.

Increased adherence to Christian denominations also involves identification of the curative forces with Christian message. It is important to note, however, that historically the Catholic ministries have enjoyed less success among the Navajo than the Protestant or even Mormon missions, due to the fact that there is an incompatibility between core Navajo religious structures and the central rites of the Catholic Church. What is involved is not only the Navajo fear of contamination with ghosts of the dead in relation to the crucifixion of Jesus, but also, the central rites of Holy Communion involve what to the Navajo are abhorrent acts of cannibalism. It remains to be seen in what manner the Navajo will be able to find ways through which the harmony and balance in their world can be maintained. Whatever resolutions or compromises are arrived at, it seems certain from past example that the people will continue to find ways through which their essential identity as Navajo is maintained.

CHRISTIAN "CONVERSION" AMONG AMERICAN INDIANS

The pervasive force of historical Christian ministries has probably had some impact upon all American Indian peoples. The gradations of Indian affiliation with Roman Catholicism and Protestant denominations span two extremes: there are those who have fully accepted the new faith, accompanied by conscious rejection of their own religious traditions and even of their own languages, and those who have been exposed to elements of Christianity, or who even may once have totally accepted Christianity, but have since returned to an often intensified participation in their own sacred ways. Incomplete evidence suggests that these two groups constitute minorities in relation to those who are situated in unique manner between the two extremes. A key element in the evaluation of Indian affiliation with Christianity, to which sufficient attention has not been given in either scholarly literature or in church documents, lies in a special meaning of conversion for most American Indians, as indeed is the case for most representatives of the primal traditions who have had contact with Christianity.

The following perspective is fundamental to this inquiry. Throughout virtually all indigenous American Indian traditions, a pervasive theme has been that all forms and forces of all orders of the immediately experienced natural environment may communicate to human beings the totality of that which is to be known of the sacred mysteries of creation, and thus of the sacred essence of being and of beings. Orally transmitted sacred lore and accompanying ritual activities that have evolved from such cumulative personal and tribal experience assure the intensification and continuity of participation in the sacred. Such conditioning to openness of mind and being toward manifestations and experiences of the sacred makes it understandable that for these peoples religious matters of whatever origin are not open to either question or argument. When, therefore, the Christian message came to the peoples through dedicated missionaries who led exemplary and sacrificial lives, the people easily understood the truths of message and example due to the profundity of their own beliefs; it was not difficult for them to adopt and adapt new expressions of values into the sacred fabric of their own religious culture. The historical phenomenon is thus not conversion as understood in exclusivistic manner by the bearers of Christianity, but rather a continuation of the people's ancient and traditional facility for what may be termed nonexclusive cumulative adhesion. If this process of polysynthesis can be accomplished with neither confusion nor dissonance, it is ultimately due to the ability of American Indian peoples to penetrate and comprehend the central and most profound nature of all experience and reality. It may therefore be affirmed that American Indian living religions have the right to a legitimate place alongside the great religious traditions of the world.

2

The Spiritual
Legacy

For centuries the American Indian peoples have been involved in a struggle that has taken on the proportions of a tragedy. It is a double tragedy, for it is ours as well as theirs, and it is still being enacted today. These original Americans have had, and fortunately still do have, great riches in human and spiritual resources. Yet these riches are either being swept aside and forgotten, or are being consciously and actively destroyed by a civilization that is out of balance precisely because it has lost those values. We give credit to the Indians for the discovery and development of foods, narcotics, and tobacco, yet we choose to forget what they never forgot, that we cannot live by bread alone. By ignoring or denying the spiritual legacy left to us by the Indians we have contributed to their impoverishment, and we have cut ourselves off from the possibility of an enrichment we desperately need.

Our consciences are relieved by a belief in such concepts as "progress," "manifest destiny," or the inevitability of our own way over all other life patterns, many of which have brought fulfillment, beauty, and dignity in a measure we cannot know so long as we continue in our present direction. In the history of humankind this conflict between cultures may be inevitable. And yet it is not inevitable that the

American Indians give up the spiritual values and ritual practices of their ancient religions. Many Indians today, even among their young people and in spite of tremendous pressures brought against them from all sides, still find strength and meaning in their own religious beliefs and ceremonies. Those who remain faithful should be given every possible encouragement, because they are helping to keep alive a rich and truly American heritage that can be found nowhere else in the world, and that can provide values sorely needed by a culture seeking purpose and direction.

For the American Indians themselves, striving to adjust to new patterns of thinking and living, it is of crucial importance to rediscover and reaffirm their own heritage, for people cannot cut themselves off from what they really are without becoming as a tree without either roots or nourishment. Among the many forces at work to mold the Indian into a new image is our educational policy, which has been perpetuating a grave error in omitting from school curriculums almost everything that could and should affirm a heritage of great value; it could even be said that the policy was intentionally designed to destroy this unique heritage, and has thus risked creating people lacking either roots or purpose.

During the early contacts between Europeans and American aborigines the Indian was either depicted as a brutal savage, without civilization and possibly without a soul, or else was painted as an innocent child of nature, a type that is nonexistent for the simple reason that humankind as a whole has lost the goodness of "paradise." The strictly ethnological accounts are of course more accurate and objective, but being a relative and specialized science, ethnology by its very nature is limited. An objective description of religious rites, social customs, or ritual paraphernalia may help us to catalogue and deduce certain conclusions but cannot give an insight into the spirituality many of the Indians knew and expressed in all facets of their culture.

As Frithjof Schuon, writing with great depth of understanding about the American Indian, has said recently:

> The fascinating combination of combative and stoical heroism and priestly bearing gave the Indian of the Plains and Forests something of the majesty of the eagle and the sun. This powerful and unique beauty of the Red Man contributes to his fame as a warrior and martyr. If none of the so-called primitive peoples have given rise to as lively and lasting an interest as have the Red Indians, and if the Indian incarnates a certain nostalgia of ours which it would be wrong to call puerile, there must be some cause for it in the Indian himself, for "where there is smoke there is fire."[1]

There are times, to be sure, when our unfamiliarity with their symbolical forms, coupled with our own ethnocentricity, cause us to doubt whether American Indians had what we call "civilization," or whether they were developed enough to worship a Supreme Being approaching that which Christianity refers to as God. With our own overemphasis on mental activity we are apt to think that the Indian, without any written language, lacks something important or necessary in not possessing a scholastic or dialectical type of doctrinal presentation. However such a "lack" may have prevented *us* from understanding the completeness and depth of their wisdom, it represents for the Indians a very effective type of spiritual participation in which the essential ideas and values, reflected by a world of forms and symbols, are spontaneously and integrally *lived*. Undoubtedly Saint Bernard expressed something of the Indian's perspective when he said:

> What I know of the divine sciences and Holy Scripture, I learnt in woods and fields. I have had no other masters than the beeches and the oaks. Listen to a man of experience: thou wilt learn more in the woods than in books. Trees and stones will teach thee more than thou canst acquire from the mouth of a magister.

A further barrier to our understanding is our deep-rooted

prejudice against the nomadic way of life many of the Indian groups followed. We are so blinded by the perspectives of our own society that we cannot realize that complex material achievements of the type we possess, or rather by which we are often possessed, are usually had at the expense of human and spiritual values. A minimum of material possessions does not necessarily mean a corresponding poverty in mental and spiritual achievements. The nomadic type of culture offers valuable lessons to the contemporary industrial person who is in danger of being crushed by the sheer weight of civilization, and who therefore often sacrifices the deepest and most meaningful values of life by identifying with an endless series of distracting and often destructive gadgets.

The material that is presented in this chapter is drawn from the traditions of the Indians of the Great Plains. The tribes of the Plains, with their unusual intellectuality, and with the great beauty and dignity of their cultural forms, represent an especially rich development among Amerindian peoples. It is not without reason that whenever the typical American Indian is to be represented it is usually the Plains Indian, with his magnificent fringed buckskin, eagle feathers, and quill decorations—all making for one of the most noble, dignified, and spectacular costumes to be found anywhere in the world. Another lifelong student of the American Indian, Hartley Burr Alexander, also emphasizes their unique position: "Under the great tutelage of Nature, noble and beautiful ceremonies were created, having at their hearts truths universal to mankind; and nowhere in America were such mysteries loftier and more impressive than among the tribes of the Great Plains."[2]

A second reason for concentrating on the Plains Indians is simply my familiarity with them. For over a year I had the opportunity of living with an old man, Black Elk (Hehaka Sapa), who was a Lakota Sioux of the Pine Ridge Reservation in South Dakota. During this year Black Elk and his close friend Little Warrior freely told me about their religion and gave me the keys to the spiritual meaning behind the forms of their rites and symbols. This new understanding made clear to me why these old men, and others among their people, manifested in their being and in every act a nobility, serenity, generosity, concentration, and kindness that we usually associate with the saints of the better-known religions. Indeed it is in these two personalities that we have proof of the efficacy and reality of the Indian's spiritual methods and values.

I first learned of Black Elk through a remarkable book recorded by John Neihardt under the title *Black Elk Speaks* (1932). But it was not until 1948, after many months of travel, that I was able to find him living with his family in a little canvas tent in a migrant potato-picking camp in Nebraska. I well remember him as he sat on an old sheepskin hide, ill and pitiful, with his almost totally blind eyes staring beyond that which surrounded him. I sat beside him for some time, and still without speaking offered him a stone pipe filled with tobacco and *kinnikinnik* in the manner that I had been taught by old men of other tribes. We smoked in silence until finally, with a soft and kindly voice, he spoke in Lakota. His son translated. He surprised me by saying that he had anticipated my coming, was glad that I was there beside him, and asked if I would remain with him, for there was much that he would like to tell me before, as he said, he would "pass from this world of darkness into the other real world of light." I therefore returned with him to his log cabin on the reservation, lived with him and his generous family for almost a year, and from him and his friends I learned about the religion of his people. Every day he talked for several hours until a veil of silence fell in which one could sense that he ws so absorbed within the realities of which he was speaking that words no longer had meaning. Indeed, the greater part of what I learned from Black Elk was not what he said, as valuable as this was, but what he was from his very being, which seemed to hover between this world of forms and the other world of the spirit.

In all that he was there radiated an atmosphere that made one feel that one was in the presence of a holy man.

Although this sanctity and wholeness was evident in other old people among the Sioux, there was in Black Elk some special quality that set him apart from his people. From the early age of nine he had received visions with an unusual frequency and intensity, so that under their power he lived with the burning compulsion to help his people by bringing back to life the "flowering tree" of their religious heritage. This tree had once flourished and borne fruit at the center of their nation, but now it had withered and Black Elk knew not what to do.

> With tears running, O Great Spirit, Great Spirit, my Grand-father—with running tears I must say now that the tree has never bloomed. A pitiful old man, you see here, and I have fallen away and have done nothing. Here at the center of the world, where you took me when I was young and taught me; here, old, I stand, and the tree is withered, Grandfather, my Grandfather!
>
> Again, and maybe the last time on this earth, I recall the great vision you sent me. It may be that some little root of the sacred tree still lives. Nourish it then, that it may leaf and bloom and fill with singing birds. Hear me, not for myself, but for my people; I am old. Hear me that they may once more go back into the sacred hoop and find the good red road, the shielding tree.[3]

Because of this mission to keep alive his religious heritage, Black Elk wished to pass on to his people and to the world those aspects of his religion that were recorded in *Black Elk Speaks*, and in the book I recorded for him in 1953, *The Sacred Pipe*. It is in keeping with his wish, and for the sake of the values themselves, that I present the following material.

One of the symbols that expresses most completely the Plains Indian concept of the relationship between human beings and the world of nature surrounding them is a cross inscribed within a circle. The symbol is painted on a number of ritual objects, and on the bodies and heads of people who participate in tribal ceremonies. Its form is reflected in the circular shape and central fire of the tipi, the Indian's home; its pattern is found in the Sun Dance and purification lodges and in many of the ritual movements. For example, in the Hako ceremony of the Pawnee, the priest draws a circle on the earth with his toe: "The circle represents a nest, and is drawn by the toe, because the Eagle [symbol of the Great Mysterious] builds its nest with its claws. Although we are imitating the bird making its nest, there is another meaning to the action; we are thinking of *Tirawa* making the world for the people to live in."[4]

In complaining that the Indian must now live in a *square* log house, a form without power to the Indians, Black Elk once said:

> You have noticed that everything an Indian does is in a circle, and that is because the Power of the World always works in circles, and everything tries to be round. In the old days when we were a strong and happy people, all our power came to us from the sacred hoop of the nation, and so long as the hoop was unbroken, the people flourished. The flowering tree was the living center of the hoop, and the circle of the four quarters nourished it. The east gave peace and light, the south gave warmth, the west gave rain, and the north with its cold and mighty wind gave strength and endurance. This knowledge came to us from the outer world with our religion. Everything the Power of the World does is done in a circle. The sky is round, and I have heard that the earth is round like a ball, and so are all the stars. The wind, in its greatest power, whirls. Birds make their nests in circles, for theirs is the same religion as ours. The sun comes forth and goes down again in a circle. The moon does the same, and both are round. Even the seasons form a great circle in their changing, and always come back again to where they were. The life of a man is a circle from childhood to childhood, and so it is in everything where power moves. Our teepees were round like the nests of birds, and these were always set in a circle, the nation's hoop, a nest of many nests, where the Great Spirit meant for us to hatch our children.[5]

At the center of the circle, uniting within a point the four directions of the cross and all the other quaternaries of the Universe, is a human person. Without the awareness that they bear within themselves this sacred center, human beings are in fact less than human. It is to recall the virtual reality of this center that the Indians have so many rites based on the cross within the circle.

One of the most precise ritual expressions of this "centrality" is found in one of the rites of the Arapaho Sun Dance, in which their Sacred Wheel is placed against each of the four sides of a man's body, starting from the feet and moving to the head, and is then turned sunwise four times, until finally it is lowered over the head, with the four attached eagle feathers hanging down over the man's breast, so that he is ritually at the center, a vertical axis to the horizontal wheel.

This concept of the vertical axis explains the sacredness of the number seven to the Indians, and it is interesting to note that their interpretation is identical to that found in other major religions. In adding the vertical dimensions of sky and earth to the four horizontal ones of space, we have six dimensions, with the seventh as the point at the center where all the directions meet.

To realize this symbol in its fullness we must conceive of three horizontal circles inscribed with crosses, all three pierced by the vertical axis of humanity itself. For the Indians understand that human beings are intermediate between sky and earth, linking the two, with feet on the ground and the head, or intellect, at the center of the firmament. The middle disc, like the vertical axis, represents humanity, for in joining sky and earth, it is neither pure spirit nor gross matter, but a synthesis of both. This particular symbol may be found among the Crow in the three rings they often paint around the sacred cottonwood tree at the center of their circular Sun Dance lodge. It was further explained to me by an old Crow priest or medicine man that these circles represent the three "worlds" that constitute human beings: body, soul, and spirit, or again: gross, subtle, and pure.

Once this concept of humanity and its relationship to the universe has been understood, one is able to understand the Indians' approach to the forms of virgin nature that surrounded them, and which they knew so intimately. In most of the great religious traditions of the world people built centers of worship in the form of cathedrals, churches, or temples, and in these centers and in the many symbolical forms introduced into them, people expressed their image of the universe. It is certainly not difficult to sense this totality, or to feel that one is actually at the center of the world when one is inside the great medieval cathedrals of Europe. For the Indians, however, the world of nature itself was their temple, and within this sanctuary they showed great respect to every form, function, and power. That the Indians held as sacred all the natural forms surrounding them is not unique, for other traditions (Japanese Shinto, for example) respect created forms as manifestations of God's works. But what is almost unique in the Indians' attitude is that their reverence for nature and for life is *central* to their religion: each form in the world around them bears such a host of precise values and meanings that taken all together they constitute what one would call their "doctrine."

In my first contacts with Black Elk almost all that he said was phrased in terms involving animals and natural phenomena. I naively wished that he would begin to talk about religious matters, until I finally realized that he was, in fact, explaining his religion. The values I sought were to be found precisely in his stories and accounts of the bison, eagle, trees, flowers, mountains, and winds.

Due to this intense preoccupation with the forms of nature, Indians have been described as being in their religion either pantheistic, idolatrous, or downright savage. It is hardly necessary to reply to the two latter terms, but the more subtle charge of pantheism, which involves equating God with manifested forms, requires some clarification.

In the extremely beautiful creation myths of the Plains Indians, which are amazingly similar to the biblical Genesis, the animals were created before human beings, so that in their anteriority and divine origin they have a certain proximity to the Great Spirit (*Wakan-Tanka* in the language of the Sioux), which demands respect and veneration. In them the Indian sees actual reflections of the qualities of the Great Spirit, which serve the same function as revealed scriptures in other religions. They are intermediaries or links between human beings and God. This explains not only why religious devotions may be directed to the deity *through* the animals, but it also helps us to understand why contact with, or from, the Great Spirit, comes to the Indian almost exclusively through visions involving animal or other natural forms. Black Elk, for example, received spiritual power (*wochangi*) from visions involving the eagle, the bison, Thunder-beings, and horses; and it is said that Crazy Horse, the great chief and holy man, received his power and invulnerability from the rock, and also from a vision of the shadow.

Although these natural forms may reflect aspects of the Great Spirit, and eventually cannot be other than the Great Spirit, they are nevertheless not identified with He "who is without Parts," and who in His transcendent unity is above all particular created forms. The Indian therefore cannot be termed a pantheist, if we accept this term in the usual sense. Black Elk has formulated well this mystery in the following statement:

> . . . We regard all created beings as sacred and important, for everything has a *wochangi,* or influence, which can be given to us, through which we may gain a little more understanding if we are attentive. We should understand well that all things are the works of the Great Spirit. We should know that

He is within all things; the trees, the grasses, the rivers, the mountains and all the four-legged animals, and the winged peoples; and even more important, we should understand that He is also above all these things and peoples.[6]

To make these distinctions more precise, it should be noted that in the language of the Sioux (Lakota), the Great Spirit may be referred to as either Father (*Ate*) or Grandfather (*Tunkashila*). Ate refers to the Great Spirit in relation to His creation, in other words, as Being, whereas Tunkashila is the nonmanifest essence, independent of the limitations of creation. These same distinctions have been enunciated by Christian theologians using the term God as distinct from Godhead, and in the Hindu doctrines that differentiate between Brahma (the masculine form) and Brahman (the neuter form).

In recalling the symbol of the circle, cross, and central axis, we can now see that although humans were created last of all the creatures, they are also the "axis," and thus in a sense the first. For if each animal reflects particular aspects of the Great Spirit, human beings, on the contrary, may include within themselves all the aspects. A human being is thus a totality, bearing the Universe within himself or herself and through the intellect having the potential capacity to live in continual awareness of this reality. As Black Elk has said: "Peace . . . comes within the souls of men when they realize their relationship, their oneness, with the universe and all its powers, and when they realize that at the center of the Universe dwells *Wakan-Tanka*, and that this center is really everywhere, it is within each of us."[7]

The Indian believes that such knowledge cannot be realized unless there is perfect humility, unless human beings humble themselves before the entire creation, before the smallest ant, realizing their own nothingness. Only in being nothing may an individual human being become everything, and only then realize the essential kinship with all forms of life. A human being's center, or Life, is the same center or Life of all that is.

Because of humankind's totality and centrality it has the almost divine function of guardianship over the world of nature. Once this role is ignored or misused people are in danger of being shown ultimately by nature who in reality is the conqueror and who the conquered. It could also be said, from another perspective, that in the past humans had to protect themselves from the forces of nature, whereas today it is nature that must be protected from humans.

Nothing is more tragic or pitiful than the statements of Indians who have survived to see their sacred lands torn up and desecrated by a people of an alien culture who, driven largely by commercial interests, have lost the sense of protective guardianship over nature. Typical are the words of an old Omaha:

> When I was a youth, the country was very beautiful. Along the rivers were belts of timberland, where grew cottonwood, maple, elm, ash, hickory, and walnut trees, and many other shrubs. And under these grew many good herbs and beautiful flowering plants. In both the woodland and the prairies I could see the trails of many kinds of animals and could hear the cheerful songs of many kinds of birds. When I walked abroad I could see many forms of life, beautiful living creatures which *Wakanda* had placed here; and these were, after their manner, walking, flying, leaping, running, playing all about. But now the face of all the land is changed and sad. The living creatures are gone. I see the land desolate and I suffer an unspeakable sadness. Sometimes I wake in the night and I feel as though I should suffocate from the pressure of this awful feeling of loneliness.[8]

Too often statements such as this are passed off as nostalgic romanticism, but if we understand the full meaning of the world of nature for the Indian, we realize that we are involved witnesses to a great tragedy, whose final act is still to be seen.

The remarkable spiritual development to be found among many of the Plains Indians derives not only from their close contact with nature, but also through rigorous participation in a multitude of rites and symbols of a supernatural origin, which are often of great complexity. Through participation in these rites, which have been faithfully transmitted from generation to generation, the Indian comes to know, to understand, and then to seek those values reflected in the great mirror of nature. Far from being simple and passive "children of nature," the Indians have dynamic personalities of great force, courage, and intelligence, and often undergo intense suffering and sacrifice in becoming what they are and in preserving what they have.

Through people such as Black Elk, Little Warrior, Standing Bear, Ohiyesa (Charles Eastman), and others, we are able to understand the wisdom in their rites and cultural forms. We know of the sacred power they individually received when they made their religious retreats (*hanble-cheyapi*), alone on high mountain tops, going for four days or more without food or water, and praying continually that the Great Spirit might hear and in compassion send one of His messengers in a vision.

In the religious retreat the Indian as an individual sought spiritual renewal, whereas in the rites of the annual spring Sun Dance (*Wiwanyag Wachipi*) the entire tribe gathered to ensure renewal not only of the participating individual, but of the tribe itself, of the world, and of the Universe. This four-day ritual dance is also still practiced by most of the Plains Indians, even though many of the forms have been modified and simplified under pressures from missionaries and the "civilizing" influences of our modern world. The essential power and functions of the Sun Dance, however, are still present, and anybody who has observed the complete three- or four-day ceremony cannot but be impressed, and deeply moved, by the otherworldly beauty of the sacred songs, by the powerful rhythm of the great drum struck simultaneously by many men, by the directness in the geometry of the ritual movements of the dancers (which again is based on the relationship between the circle and its axis or center), and by the aspects of duration and sacrifice.

To illustrate in some detail at least one of the Plains Indians ceremonies I have chosen the purification rites of the sweat lodge, the *Inipi*. These rites are carried out in preparation for all the other major rites, and actually are participated in prior to any important undertaking. They are rites of renewal, or spiritual rebirth, in which each of the four elements—earth, air, fire, and water—contribute to the people's physical and psychical purification.

A small dome-shaped lodge is first made of bent willow saplings over which are placed buffalo hides, which make the little house tight and dark inside. Within the lodge, and at its center, there is a small pit containing rocks that have already been heated in a fire outside the lodge to the east. When the leader of the ceremony sprinkles water on these they give off steam, so that soon the lodge becomes intensely hot, and also fragrant from the aromatic sage strewn on the floor. Each of the materials in the lodge has its symbolic value, as does every detail of design and ritual usage.

Black Elk, among others, has explained that the lodge itself represents the Universe, with the pit at the center as the navel in which dwells the Great Spirit with His power, which is the fire. The willows that form the frame of the house represent all that grows from Mother Earth.

> These too have a lesson to teach us, for in the fall their leaves die and return to the earth, but in the spring they come to life again. So, too, men die but live again in the real world of *Wakan-Tanka,* where there is nothing but the spirits of all things; and this true life we may know here on earth if we purify our bodies and minds, thus coming closer to *Wakan-Tanka* who is all-purity.[9]

The rocks represent the earth, and also the indestructible

and everlasting nature of *Wakan-Tanka*. The water, too, reflects values for the people to learn from:

> When we use water in the sweat lodge we should think of *Wakan-Tanka* who is always flowing, giving His power and life to everything; we should even be as water which is lower than all things, yet stronger even than the rocks.[10]

It is important to note that to the Plains Indian the material form of the symbol is not thought of as representing some *other* and higher reality, but *is* that reality in an image. The power or quality, therefore, that a particular form reflects may be transferred directly to the person in contact with it, and there is no need, as with modern Western people, for any mental or artificial "reconstruction." It may even be said that the Indian can be passive to the form, and is thus able to absorb, and become on with, its reflected power.

During the four periods of sweating within the lodge, prayers are recited, sacred songs are sung, and a pipe is ceremonially smoked four times by the circle of people. At the conclusion of the fourth and last period the door is opened so that "the light enters into the darkness, that we may see not only with our two eyes, but with the one eye which is of the heart, and with which we see and know all that is true and good." Going forth into the light from the house of darkness, in which all impurities have been left behind, represents human liberation from ignorance, from the ego, and from the cosmos. The person is now a renewed being entering symbolically into the world of light or wisdom.

There is in these rites an amazing completeness. In other great religions one, or sometimes two, of the elements are used for purification or consecration. Here four of the elements are present (one could include the fifth "element": ether) in such a powerfully interrelated manner that one cannot but believe that for each participating individual the goal, in varying degrees, must be achieved.

As a thread binds together, and is central to, each bead of a necklace, so is the sacred pipe central to all the Plains Indian ceremonies. The pipe is a portable altar, and a means of grace, that every Indian once possessed. He would not undertake anything of importance unless he had first smoked, concentrating on all that the pipe represented, and thus absorbing a multitude of powers. It could in fact be said that if one could understand all the possible meanings and values to be found in the pipe and its accompanying ritual, then one could understand Plains Indian religion in its full depth.

The origin of the pipe is expressed in various myths of great beauty. In the Sioux myth a miraculous Buffalo Cow Woman brought the pipe to the people, with explanations concerning its meaning and use. Pipes used in historical times, and still used today, are made with a red, or sometimes a black, stone bowl, a stem usually of ash, and—at least with the large ceremonial types—ribbon decorations representing the four directions of space, and parts taken from sacred animals or from nature. These pipes represent the human being in his totality, or the universe of which humankind is a reflection. The bowl is the heart, or sacred center, and each section of the pipe is usually identified with some part of the human being.

As the pipe is filled with the sacred tobacco, prayers are offered for all the powers of the universe, and for the myriad forms of creation, each of which is represented by a grain of tobacco. The filled pipe is thus Totality, so that when the fire of the Great Spirit is added, a divine sacrifice is enacted in which the Universe and humankind are reabsorbed within the Principle, and become what in reality they are. In mingling life-breath with the tobacco and fire through the straight stem of concentration, the person who smokes assists at the sacrifice of the self or ego, and is thus aided in realizing the Divine Presence at his or her own center. Indeed, in the liberation of the smoke one is helped not only to find God's presence within, but to realize that oneself and the world are mysteriously plunged in God. The smoke that rises to the heavens is also, as it were, visible prayer, at the sight and fragrance of which the entire creation rejoices. The mysteries of the peace pipe are so profound that the rite of smoking for the Indian can be compared to the Holy Communion for Christians. It is therefore not without reason that it is commonly called a "peace pipe," and was always used in establishing a relationship, or peace, between friends and also enemies. For in smoking the pipe together each person is aided in remembering his or her own center, which is now understood to be the same center of every other person, and of the Universe itself. It would be difficult to imagine a rite that could more aptly express the bond that exists among all forms of creation.

All true spiritual progress involves three stages, which are not successfully experienced and left behind, but rather each in turn is realized and then integrated within the next stage, so that ultimately they become one in the individual who attains the ultimate goal. Different terms may be used for these stages, but essentially they constitute purification, perfection or expansion, and union.

If union with Truth (which is one of many possible names for God) is the ultimate goal of all spiritual disciplines, then it is evident that what is impure cannot be united with that which is all purity. Hence the necessity for the first stage of purification. Expansion follows because only that which is perfect, total, or whole can be united with absolute perfection and holiness. One must cease to be a part, an imperfect fragment; one must also realize what one really is so as to expand to include the Universe within oneself. Only then, when these two conditions of purification and expansion are actualized, may one attain to the final stage of union. All the great religions attest that there is no greater error to which human beings are subject than to regard the real self as nothing more than the body or the mind. It is only through traditional disciplines, such as those that have been described for the Plains Indian, that people are able to dispel this greatest of all illusions.

The pattern of the three stages in spiritual development may be recognized in one form or another in the methods of all the great religions of the world. It is evident that the American Indian, or at least the Plains Indian, also possesses this same threefold pattern of realization. If this spirituality has not as yet been fully recognized as existing among the Indians, it is due partly to a problem of communication, since their conceptions are often expressed through symbolic forms that are foreign to us. If we can understand, however, the truths the Indians find in their relationships to nature, and the profound values reflected by their many rites and symbols, then *we* may become enriched, our understanding will deepen, and we shall be able to give to the American Indian heritage its rightful place among the great spiritual traditions of humankind. Further, if Indians themselves can become more actively aware of this valuable heritage, then they may regain much of what has been lost, and will be able to face the world with the pride and dignity that should rightfully be theirs.

3

The Roots
of Renewal

There is an unprecedented explosion of interest today in all facets of the Native American heritage. It is especially significant that this interest and concern are shared by the Native American and the non-Native American alike. Analyses of the complex reasons for this concern is outside the scope of this book. But it may be suggested that what underlies it all is the Native American's increasing disenchantment with the world that for centuries has been presented as the ultimate model of true civilization. Paralleling this disenchantment of Native Americans is the non-Native Americans' questioning of many of the basic premises of their own civilization. Both Indian and non-Indian are engaged in a quest for the roots of lost heritages now increasingly understood to be essential if we are to reorient our cultures and lives toward values that express real human nature. In this mutual quest many Native American groups are far closer to their sources than are non-Natives. And so perhaps for the first time in history we are allowing, even asking them to talk, so that we may listen and learn. Hope lies in the possibility of a true dialogue wherein each may learn from the other, so that each may come to know himself or herself. We are essentially all engaged in the same kind of process, each in our own way asking the same kinds of fundamental questions.

The causes for the new search for the roots of lost traditions, and for self-examination and reevaluation, are at once both simple and vastly complex. They are obvious yet elusive. But if the root causes of the situation are grasped, or at least partially identified, it may be possible better to understand a multitude of present events, movements, and phenomena that are unfolding with increasing intensity. New manifestations of Indian militancy may be responsible for increased public awareness. But such action-oriented movements certainly neither define nor resolve the root causes of the problems. It would thus be superficial to assert, as has often been suggested, that action-oriented techniques are primarily responsible for the current renewal or reformulation of elements of a people's traditional heritage.

Many Native American groups have learned over generations of bitter experiences to preserve their sacred traditions underground. Some of the current "renewal," therefore, simply represents the current willingness of the people to give greater visibility to their sacred rites and beliefs, which have been kept hidden from a materially dominant world intent on destroying these very traditions.

It seems to me that we are faced today with a pervasive process, on a global scale, of detraditionalization or despiritualization. The world has been experiencing this process in a cumulative manner for many centuries. Exceedingly complex historical causes are no doubt responsible. As this process of detraditionalization has proceeded, its influence has demanded that the basic premises and orientations of our society be reevaluated. Detraditionalization has had an impact on the integrity of virtually all Native American traditions or lifeways. The reevaluation by Native American peoples of their own conditions involves an assessment of their relationships to the materially dominant society. Frequently, when sincere attempts are made by Native Americans to adjust to or acculturate within the dominant society, they become involved in a process of diminishing returns, or reach dead ends with regard to acquiring a meaningful quality of life.

The struggle of both Indians and non-Indians to find answers to their respective situations has led increasingly to attempts to regain contact with the roots of their traditions. Since their indigenous traditions are deeply and intricately rooted in this very land, unlike the more recently transplanted Europeans, the Indians have a certain advantage in this quest. It is understandable that non-Native people—especially among the younger generations—who once looked everywhere except to their own homeland for answers are now increasingly turning to Native Americans and their traditions for possible alternatives to the values of their own society. To them these values have come to represent an impoverished reality. The great hope in this dual search of Indians and non-Indians is that a true and open dialogue may be established through which neither will attempt to imitate the other, but where each may ultimately regain and reaffirm the sacred dimensions of *their own* respective traditions.

In spite of the vast differences among the sacred traditions of the native cultures of North America, it is nevertheless possible to identify certain core or root themes that seem to undergird the traditions of all these groups, even though they are expressed through a rich diversity of means.

TIME

Within traditional Native American cultures, time tends to be experienced as cyclical and rhythmic rather than as linear and "progress"-oriented. The rhythm of the world in its mode of operation is believed to be circular, as is the life of a human or of any manifested form or being. Events or processes transmitted through oral traditions tend not to be recounted in terms of time past or time future in the linear sense. Indeed most Native American languages do not have past and future tenses; they reflect rather a perennial reality of the now. The rich mythic accounts of creation, for example, do not tell of chronological time past, but of processes that are eternally happening. The same processes are recurring now and are to recur in other future cycles.

Given this structure of experience that is supported by the forms of language and made immediate through experienced interrelationships with the elements of each people's natural environment, it is impossible in Native American thought to conceive of progress in the non-Indian linear sense—that quantitatively interpreted cumulative process in which the more and the new are mysteriously and automatically identified with the better. However, the forces and events asserting themselves upon us at this moment in our history increasingly demand a backward look at progress so that its premises may be reexamined critically. Through such reexamination and, possibly, reorientation, Native American traditions may serve as a reminder of forgotten or neglected dimensions latent within European America's own heritage. For example, we know that at one time this heritage also manifested a dependence on sacred time.

PLACE

If alternatives are being sought today to our pervasive linear, progress-laden concepts of time, there is also the parallel quest for a new understanding and appreciation of place. Native American affirmations of the interrelated sacredness of time and place are spelled out across our land with enormous creative diversity. Yet all of it exhibits some fundamental common principles.

Native American experiences of place are infused with mythic themes. These express events of sacred time, which are as real now as at any other time. They are experienced through landmarks in each people's immediate natural environment. The events of animal beings, for example, which are communicated through oral traditions of myths or folklore, serve to grace, sanctify, explain, and interpret each detail of the land. Further, each being of nature, every particular form of the land, is experienced as the locus of qualitatively differentiated spirit beings, whose individual and collective presence sanctifies and gives meaning to the land in all its details and contours. Thus, it also gives meaning to the lives of people who cannot conceive of themselves apart from the land. Such beliefs in a plurality of indwelling spirits (often referred to rather unkindly as "animism" or "animatism") must be understood in relation to a polysynthetic quality of vision. The recognition of multiplicity on one level of reality need not militate against the coalescing of the omnipresent spirit beings within a more ultimate unitary principle. Such a polysynthetic metaphysic of nature, immediately experienced rather than dangerously abstracted, speaks with particular force to the root causes of many of today's problems, especially to our present so-called ecological crisis. It is perhaps this message of the sacred nature of the land, of place, that today has been most responsible for forcing the Native American vision upon the mind and conscience of the non-Native American.

Such affirmation and experience of sacred time and sacred place wherever these may be found tend to free humanity from the oppressive limits of profane time and profane place. Experiencing such constriction and thus inevitably feeling nostalgia for what has been lost, people today have come to seek the illusion of liberation through explorations of outer space. This quest is futile, of course, especially if embarked upon to satisfy ultimate concerns, since even such seemingly limitless reaches of space, being always of a material and thus quantitative order, are still within the domain of limitation. Such attempts by contemporary humans to "conquer" time and space, even to "conquer" specific places, are incomprehensible to Native Americans, particularly to Native American or arctic shamans. These shamans through the nonmaterial means of their sacred traditions are able to travel at will through the freedom of sacred space unfettered by mechanical, profane time.

Not only Native Americans but traditional-oriented peoples, wherever they may be, always found the means by which to be protected from the indefiniteness of space. The tipi, the hogan, or the longhouse—like the temple, the cathedral, or the sacred city center of antiquity—determined the perimeters of space in such a way that a sacred place, or enclosure, was established. Space so defined served as a model of the world, of the universe, or, microcosmically, of a human being. Essential to such definition of space, so central to human need, were means by which the centers of sacred space or place were established. For without such ritual fixing of a center there can be no circumference. And with neither circumference nor center where does a person stand? A ritually defined center, whether the fire at the center of the Plains tipi or the *sipapu* (earth navel) within the Pueblo kiva, obviously expresses not just a mathematically fixed point established arbitrarily in space. It is also taken to be the actual center of the world. It is understood as an axis serving as a bridge between heaven and earth, an axis that pierces through a multiplicity of worlds. The great cottonwood tree at the center of (and branching out above) the Plains Sun Dance lodge is this central axis. It symbolizes the way of liberation from the limits of the cosmos. Vertical ascent is impossible unless the starting point is the ritual center. Here again such primordial types of formulations found within our American land may serve as reminders to those who have lost or forgotten the sense of a center.

RELATIONSHIP

One key to the Native American religious perspective, which again speaks to a quality of life sought by contemporary generations in their loss of center and concomitant sense of alienation and fragmentation, may be found in Native American concepts of relationship, all orders of which are richly defined and supported by the forms of language and by specific ritual means. Relationships between members of family, band, clan, or tribal groups tend to be defined, and thus intensified, through relational or generational terms rather than through personal names which are considered to be sacred and thus private to the individual. This sense of relationship pertains not only to members of a nuclear family, band, or clan. It also extends outward to include all beings of the specific environment, the elements, and the winds, whether these beings, forms, or powers are what we would call animate or inanimate. In Native American thought no such hard dichotomies exist. All such forms under creation are understood to be mysteriously interrelated. Everything is relative to every other being or thing; thus, nothing exists in isolation. The intricately interrelated threads of the spider's web are used as a metaphor for the world. The same reference occurs in Native American art. This is a profound symbol, when it is understood. The people observed that the threads of the web were drawn out from within the spider's very being. They also recognized that the threads in concentric circles were sticky, whereas the threads leading to the center were smooth!

One vivid example of this comprehensive sense of relationship is expressed with special force among the Plains peoples in rites involving communal smoking of the pipe. At the conclusion of the pipe ceremony among the Lakota the participants all exclaim: "We are all related!" What is acknowledged here is not only the relatedness of the immediate participating group. There is also an affirmation of the mysterious interrelatedness of all that is. The rites of the pipe specifically mention that each of the indefinite number of grains of tobacco placed in the bowl of the pipe represents ritually, or really *is*, some specific form or possibility of creation. The act of smoking then is a rite of communion. Through the agency of human breath the apparent multiplicity and separateness of phenomena (the tobacco) is absorbed within an ultimate unity (the fire).

If new life is being given to such rites as communal pipe-smoking among Native American peoples today, or to any similar means for the reaffirmation of relationship, belonging, and identity, it is entirely understandable. Many Native Americans are drawn to such expressions because they have either been denied truly meaningful relationships with the dominant society, or have found frustration in a society where experience is so excessively and artificially fragmented.

THE ORAL TRADITIONS

Perhaps the greatest tragedy to come upon Native American groups has been the progressive weakening and occasional total loss of their respective languages. Since language supports and communicates the total range of a people's values and world view, it was realized early by the dominant society that Native American languages must be supplanted by the language of the dominant society if cultural assimilation was to occur. The history of the frequent brutal means by which this process of deculturation was furthered need not be reiterated here. We must stress the fact, however, that due to the inherent persistence of language many Native American languages have survived. Furthermore, many Native American groups are taking deliberate measures to insure that these languages are both recovered and used.

These procedures are being assisted by the increasing control Native Americans are exercising with respect to their own educational systems. Where such languages are alive, oral traditions can be revitalized to communicate the core values to all members of the group. Some segments of the dominant society, which has always placed a very high premium on literacy and on the linear perspective—in this case the written line—have finally begun to recognize the powerful effectiveness of oral transmission for educational purposes. The importance given to the "frame"—that is, the time, the season, and the immediate environment within which the narration takes place—serves to place, reinforce, and intensify what is communicated. Regardless of the type of myth or folktale, multiple levels of understanding are always possible. This enables the narration to speak specifically and simultaneously to all age groups present. Normally in tribal societies the elders of experience serve as repositories for the oral lore of the people. Living oral traditions give the elders of the society a position of respect and importance. Further, since oral tradition speaks even to the youngest in the group, it creates bridges of understanding between the generations. Oral tradition can thus be addressed with special force to problems of generational segmentation and individual alienation so typical of much of the American world today.

It is a trait of the Southwestern Pueblo peoples to objectify the realities and dynamics of experience through the *kachinas,* sometimes called "gods." There is an account of a Zuni kachina who emerged from the underworld attached back to back with a person from an alien world. Back to back, it was suggested, the alien is destined neither to see nor to understand the Zuni. Yet the fact remains that the two are attached. If there is hope, it lies in the possibility that there may come a time for a turning around, so that each may know who the other is and what the other might become.

4

The Persistence
of Essential Values

To examine the complex question of the persistence of essential traditional values among American Indian groups, we shall focus on the Indians of the Great Plains of North America. This selection in a sense is arbitrary, for similar studies could well be extended to almost any of the American Indian groups scattered in reservations throughout the United States, many of whom still retain, underneath the more evident surface changes and adaptations, world views and lifeways still deeply rooted in ancient values. Since my closest personal contacts, however, have been with the Plains tribes such as the Sioux, Cheyenne, Crow, Blackfoot, Arapaho, and Shoshone, I have chosen to look to these cultures for evidence of persistence of essential traditional values.

The use of the term "essential values" in this context refers to transcendent metaphysical principles central to the spiritual ways of the Plains Indians, which constitute for these original Americans an expression of what has been called the *religio perennis*. The uniqueness, or possibly strangeness, to us of the Indian's ritual forms or symbolical language should never blind us to the universal quality of the underlying values themselves. The survival of the values themselves is not in question, for being ultimately timeless and eternal they can never in themselves be qualified by the vicissitudes of the sociocultural environment. The question, rather, is the degree to which changes imposed by an alien and generally profane culture will allow these values to continue to operate within a changing cultural matrix and thus within the human substance of the individual.

This chapter will first describe selected indigenous core values of the Plains Indians as they are conveyed through their ritual supports, and thus as they contribute to methods of spiritual realization. This necessarily synthetic treatment provides a reference base for the second part of the chapter, which will deal with several dimensions in the dynamics of contact, as the indigenous culture confronts the pervasive and disruptive influences issuing from a materially dominant Anglo-American culture.

VALUES

Among the many sacred ceremonies of the Plains Indians, three major rituals—separately and in their totality—exemplify all necessary dimensions of a true way of spiritual realization for the individual and for the social group as a whole. These rites are those of purification, the annual tribal Sun Dance, and the individual spiritual retreat.

The rites of purification, considered to be essential preparation for any important or sacred undertaking, have been described to some extent on p. 42. To elaborate further, the domed shaped sweat lodge is said to symbolize the very body of the Great Spirit. Inside this lodge participants submit themselves to intensely hot steam. As the people pray and chant, the steam, actually conceived as the visible image of the Great Spirit, acts as in an alchemical work to dissolve both physical and psychic "coagulations" so that a spiritual transmutation may take place. The four elements, with the invisible spiritual Presence—or "fifth element"—contribute their respective powers to this purifying process so that the individual may become truly whole by first dissolving the illusory sense of separateness, then becoming reintegrated, or harmoniously unified, within the totality of the universe. In finally going forth from the dark lodge, leaving behind all physical impurities and spiritual errors, a person is reborn into the wisdom of the light of day. All aspects of the world have been witnesses to this cycle of corruption, death, wholeness, and rebirth; indeed, the cosmic powers have all contributed to the process.

In the rites of the Sun Dance (see pp. 16 and 41) there is a shift in perspective and function. These dramatic and powerful rites, normally of four days' duration, are generally performed only once annually, and are participated in, directly or indirectly, by the entire tribal group. A major overt goal of this prayer dance is the regeneration or renewal not only of the individual directly participating in the rites, but also of the tribe and ultimately of the entire universe.

Blowing on whistles made from the wing bone of the eagle, the men dance individually with simple and dignified steps toward the central tree from which they receive supernatural power, and then dance backward to the periphery of the circle without shifting their gaze from the center. The sacred forms and ritual actions are virile, dignified, and direct. The power of the sacred center, now realized within the people themselves, remains throughout the year with each individual and contributes to their unity.

The third spiritual way is the solitary retreat known as the "lamenting," or the vision quest. In this quest the individual, naked and alone, and in constant prayer, endures a total fast for a specified number of days at a lonely place, usually a mountain top. In utter humility of body and mind, often emphasized by the offering of pieces of his flesh or the joint of a finger, the individual stands before the forms and forces of nature seeking the blessing of sacred power which should come to him through a dream, or preferably a vision, of some aspect of nature, possibly an animal, who offers guidance for the future direction of the individual's life. These natural forms or forces, conceived as messengers or agents, constitute for the Indian a well-understood "iconography" in which forms, with their accompanying powers, are ranked according to their ability to express most directly the ultimate Power, or essence, of the Great Spirit. Essential to this metaphysic of nature is the Indian's belief that in silence, found within the solitude of nature, there is ultimately heard the very voice of the Great Spirit. This quest for supernatural power, symbolically coming from the "outside" but in reality being awakened from within, has always been essential to the spiritual life of Plains Indian men and women, and its influence on the quality of their lives should never be underestimated.

Finally, mention must be made of the sacred tobacco pipe which is an important ritual implement central to all three rites. In this portable altar the Indian has access at all times to an effective synthetic support for spiritual realization. The rites of the pipe express sacrifice and purification; they affirm the integration of the individual within the macrocosm, and they lead finally to the realization of unity, prefigured by the totality of the grains of tobacco becoming one with the fire of the Great Spirit.

There may be discerned in these spiritual ways of purification a pattern for which parallels may be found in virtually all the legitimate methods of spiritual realization within the world's great religions. This universal pattern affirms the sequence first of purification, followed by an expansive process in the realization of totality, or the state of human perfection, leading finally to the ultimate possibility of contact and identity with the one transcendent supreme principle.

CONTACT: DYNAMICS OF THE ACCULTURATION PROCESS

Is it possible today for small minority groups within the United States, or anywhere for that matter, to retain the integrity of cultural patterns and spiritual ways similar to those just described—ways rooted in traditions of primordial origin which had their essential supports in a world of nature still virgin and unscarred by the hand of any human being?

All the forces of historical contact between the American Indian and the materially dominant Euro-American civilization seem to be totally against the possibility of any traditional continuity for the Indian. The power of alien forces and the inevitable disruption of lifeways that has ensued must not be minimized. The people's subsistence base, the bison, was brought to near extinction through commercial exploitation combined with an avowed policy of extermination by the United States Army. Freedom of movement was restricted by force to reservations often arbitrarily chosen.

Governing techniques based on the accumulated wisdom of the elders were replaced by an imposed bureaucratic system, which could never, even if it wished, understand the real problems of the people under its charge. In accord with the Euro-American concept of ownership, the random distribution of parcels of land on the basis of individual family units shattered the cohesive unity of the Indian's own larger consanguineous groupings, and the prohibition of plural marriages disrupted the immediate family units. School systems were imposed that had as their avowed goals the suppression and eventual elimination of traditional values in order to hasten forcefully the process of total assimilation. This policy, with all too few exceptions, is still basic to today's school system on the reservation. Ill-conceived government attempts at economic rehabilitation have ended again and again in total failure largely due to the fact that agriculture, then identified by white people with civilization, was a practice contradictory to all Indian values, which held the earth as sacred and inviolate and not to be torn up with a plow. Among the most difficult trials, however, were the hostile attitudes toward the Indian's religious practices. Sacrificial elements of the Sun Dance were prohibited, as were the rites held for the departing souls of the dead, and it is well known how participation in the much-misunderstood Ghost Dance ended in the infamous massacre of Wounded Knee in 1890.

This series of traumatic shocks received by the Indian is obviously not just the inevitable result of straightforward military defeats, as devastating as these were, but rather the tragic drama of two cultures in conflict, each representing to the other diametrically opposed values on every possible level and in all domains. Such conflict between cultures was undoubtedly intensified by the fact that those segments of Euro-American society with which the Indian had the most contact were, with few exceptions, probably the least enlightened carriers of the more positive facets of "civilization." With the exception of some Christian missionaries of "good heart," the Indians found no segment of American society with which they could identify themselves.

After more than a century of this bitter confrontation with accompanying disruptions in social, economic, political, and religious life, it is difficult to understand how the people have survived at all. Yet the Plains Indians, as well as other groups, have survived with tenacity and even vitality that certain rites and ceremonies are actually undergoing renewed affirmation. Much to the surprise of the social scientists and the Bureau of Indian Affairs itself, the "vanishing American" has somehow not vanished at all. It had been incorrectly assumed, among other factors, that just as so many European immigrants had readily assimilated into the great American "melting pot," so too would the Indian. There was obviously a failure to take into account the tremendous differences between the European and the American Indian. The result of this new awareness, on the part of anthropologists at least, has led to a growing number of hypotheses to explain the phenomenon of the tenacity of traditional values and cultures.

One such hypothesis has pointed to the isolation of the reservations. This is undoubtedly an important factor, yet it must be recalled that for certain groups—the Mohawk, for example, who construct skyscrapers in New York City—close and frequent contact has not resulted in the total abandonment of ancient values. The sustaining power of culture-bearing indigenous languages has been reflected in the literature; certainly it has been well understood by the reservation school systems, which to this day often forbid children, under threat of punishment, to speak their own native language.

It has been suggested, with reason, that the policies of forced or "directed" acculturation to which all Indian groups have been subjected lead to violent reactions that reject change and reaffirm traditionalism. A converse possibility neglected by the specialists has been the role of the half-informed, usually sentimental "Indian lovers," the "do-gooders," who would preserve certain of the "more noble" Indian values while incorporating such modern innovations as housing and hygiene. Paradoxically, these seemingly sympathetic approaches may be far more corrosive to traditional values than the uncompromising ethnocentric attitudes of those who insist on total assimilation, by force if necessary.

Among the vast array of forces that work for the persistance of traditional values is the often neglected psychological factor of the inherent stability of the basic personality structure, which acts as a selective screen in processes of change. A dimension central to this complex question, but inaccessible to the quantitative experiential tools of either cultural anthropology or psychology, is the qualitative power of metaphysical, or cosmological, principles and the degree to which these become virtual or effective within the individual substance through participation in traditional rites and spiritual methods. Related to this entire question of the quality of personality is the fact that where Indians are still able to live in an area of as-yet-unspoiled nature, potentially they have access to a vast array of transcendent values. For this potential source to become virtual, however, the Indian must still possess, to a certain degree at least, the traditional metaphysic of nature. Where this metaphysic is still understood, and can be directly related to the supporting forms of the natural world, the Indian has here perhaps the strongest ally in preserving essential values. It is also in this metaphysic of nature that we find the Indian's most valuable message for the contemporary world.

A final factor relating to the persistence of values is crucial today to a multitude of problems deriving from attitudes in America toward minority groups of various ethnic backgrounds. Euro-American racial attitudes have historically so tended to devaluate physical types of other cultural traditions that these peoples generally have been relegated to positions of inferior status in the larger society. In thus being denied the possibility of social or cultural mobility, many of these groups have tended to seek cohesion and identity through reaffirmation of their own traditional values. The resulting low index of intermarriage between these minority groups and the dominant majority has also tended to slow acculturation. (This situation, incidentally, has not occurred in Mexico, where positive valuation has been given to the Indian heritage.) Among the ramifications of negative racist attitudes is that many Indians who do attempt to assimilate into segments of Euro-American culture tend to undergo a cycle of progressive disenchantment, a process often hastened by the slum conditions of cities or by participation in foreign wars. When such persons then attempt to reintegrate themselves into their own traditional societies they often serve as powerful agents for the preservation of traditional values.

CONTEMPORARY ASSESSMENT

Several centuries of direct contact of the diverse Plains Indian groups with Euro-Americans has resulted in such a broad spectrum of adjustments, conservative reactions, or total changes that it is obviously impossible to make valid generalizations in terms of the contemporary persistence of values. Within this spectrum of multiple possibilities there are examples, across groups as well as within particular groups, of near-total retention of traditional values at the one end of the scale to near-total assimilation at the other end. The vast majority of groups or individuals, however, probably lie in the mid-range and generally represent a more or less synthetic reassemblage of Indian and Euro-American values, always with the retention, however, of a remarkable degree of traditional Indianness.

Available data indicate that concordant with a high degree of traditional persistence a culture generally has cohesiveness and direction and affords personal dignity. Assimilation, on the contrary, can often represent acculturation into the lowest and least enlightened segments of Euro-American society. This can be the first step leading to extreme cultural disintegration, producing the dangerous phenomenon of a decultured people living precariously in a vacuum, unable to identify either with Indianness or with any of the Euro-American values.

In viewing the degree of cultural wreckage strewn today across the prairies, it is impressive and hopeful that so many of the core indigenous values, with their supporting rites, are generally persisting among most Plains groups. In spite of the virtual disappearance of a host of minor rites, still being practiced are the rites of purification, the Sun Dance, the spiritual retreat, and the rites of the sacred pipe. Sacred arrows, the original sacred pipe, and sacred bundles in general are still being kept with reverence and respect, even though some of the spiritual meanings of these forms may have been lost. One of the most notable aspects of these examples of traditional tenacity is the fact that those who today affirm these forms and values are not necessarily just the "long hairs," the old men; there is a growing interest and participation on the part of the younger generations as well.

An outstanding example of the contemporary process of reaffirmation is the increasing participation throughout the Plains in the Sun Dance. Among the complex factors contributing to this revitalization, which cannot be explained here in detail, is the example and stimulus afforded by a dynamic series of interpersonal and intercultural relationships between the Crow Indians of Montana and the Shoshone of Wyoming. The renewed interest among the younger generations may be partly because the youths have not been able to find channels in white society for the expression of specific needs, personal qualities, or virtues, which had always been central, and which still are relevant, to the indigenous cultures. Public display of personal courage, sacrifice, and generosity, for example, are key Indian themes dramatically affirmed in the context of the Sun Dance.

Although the three- or four-day total fast required in the Sun Dance is still observed, the self-torture features have not been publicly participated in since the government prohibitions of 1890. Such tortures, however, are still engaged in secretly by certain individuals. Also little known to outside groups is the fact that the spiritual retreat is frequently used today not only by the old, but also by the young. It is evident, although it has not been specifically mentioned, that crucial to the spiritual ways that have been mentioned is the presence of the shaman or medicine man. Judging partly from the frequency and popularity of *yuwipi* rites, which allow for the ritual demonstration of shamanistic powers, it appears that shamanism still plays a meaningful role among the people and that it continues to have mechanisms for the transmission of power. The high personal quality and magnetism of many of these people are very strong contributing factors to the holding power of traditional values.

The true nature of a growing number of pan-Indian movements, or what I call the powwow syndrome, still remains questionable, for the stimulus behind many of the movements is a reaction to Euro-American attitudes toward ethnic minorities. In being rejected the Indian affirms his or her Indianness, yet in doing this often seeks to identify with the white person's image of what an Indian is—or should be. The result is a complex of heterogeneous forms and practices that have popular appeal and commercial advantage, but that risk sacrificing true spiritual content. The extraordinary growth of the new Black Elk Sweat Lodge Organization, with membership cards and all, is undoubtedly a good example of this double-edged phenomenon of pan-Indianism.

Will educational policy, which for so long has been dictated to the Indian, honor and support indigenous values and lifeways so that the young may grow with a rightful pride in their own heritage? Or must the schools continue in their efforts toward total assimilation, thus denying Indians their birthright and robbing the larger American culture of the possibility of a spiritual enrichment that present crises indicate is so desperately needed?

Cannot Indian lands be allowed to remain inviolate, so that a unique religious heritage may continue to retain its supports in a world of sacred natural forms? Or must policies for rapid termination of protective mechanisms continue so that remaining Indian-held lands will melt away under the pressures of often unscrupulous commerical interests?

But above all, and crucial to these and many other questions: Can it not be affirmed that all peoples, regardless of skin color, ethnic background, or religious affiliation, are rightful members of one family of humankind? Should not differences of appearance, culture, or religion be affirmed as valid and even necessary expressions of a greater Reality, so that they may contribute to a richer world? Any alternative cannot but lead to drab mediocrity and ultimate chaos.

Whatever the outcome, we might well heed the words attributed to a great Indian after whom one of our cities was named, Seattle.

> We are two distinct races with separate origins and separate destinies. To us the ashes of our ancestors are sacred and their resting place is hallowed ground. You wander far from the graves of your ancestors and seemingly without regret.
> . . .
> But why should I mourn at the untimely fate of my people? Tribe follows tribe and nation follows nation, and regret is useless. . . .
> But when the last Red man shall have become a myth among the White man . . . when your children's children think themselves alone in the field . . . or in the silence of the pathless woods, they will not be alone . . . your hands will throng with the returning hosts that once filled them and still love this beautiful land. The White man will never be alone.
> Let him be just and deal kindly with my people for the dead are not powerless. Dead—I say? There is no death. Only a change of worlds.[1]

❖ 5 ❖

Contemplation
Through Action

W hat we refer to as religion cannot, in the case of the
American Indian, be separated from the forms and
dynamics of everyday life, or from almost any facet of the
total culture; nor, as we shall see more clearly, may there be
separation from the phenomena of the natural environment.
This situation is typical of religious traditions that still remain close to their primal origins and have subsisted at a
technological level that does not allow alienation from the
environment. One cannot, therefore, find in these cultures
the kinds of systematic theological structures that have become central to most of the historical religions. We could
distill out and formulate such structures, since they are latently there, but the people themselves do not overtly make
such abstractions from life and experienced reality. Religious concepts and values are given substance through the
direct visual or pictorial image and through the symbol,
which includes the auditory word or echo, all of which have
reference always to the forms, forces, and voices of nature.

A further barrier to understanding primitive traditions
may be that within the context of the historical and generally monotheistic religions, only two mutually exclusive
theistic possibilities seem to be affirmed. That is, religions
are either monotheistic or polytheistic, and generally mono-

theism has been taken as the sign of advancement in civilization. Primitive religions, however, and specifically here the American Indian traditions, do not fit into either one of these categories. Rather, these traditions represent a form of theism wherein concepts of both monotheism and polytheism intermingle and fuse without being confused. Among the western Lakota and eastern Dakota of the Plains, for example, the term *Wakan-Tanka*, Great Mysterious is an all-inclusive concept that refers both to a Supreme Being and to the totality of all gods or spirits or powers of creation. Such conceptualizations embracing both unity and diversity are typical of the polysynthetic nature of the languages of these peoples, and thus of their modes of conceptualization and cognitive orientations. Black Elk was able to affirm: "Wakan-Tanka, you are everything, and yet above everything." Abundant recorded materials make it evident beyond any doubt that this type of ultimate affirmation of a Supreme Being was held before the coming of white people and Christian missionaries, not only among the Lakota, but among most, if not all, American Indian peoples. The contemporary Navajo artist Carl Gorman, speaking from a culture very different from that of the Plains people, has recently written:

> It has been said by some researchers into Navajo religion, that we have no Supreme God, because He is not named. That is not so. The Supreme Being is not named because He is unknowable. He is simply the Unknown Power. We worship him through His Creation. We feel too insignificant to approach directly in prayer that Great Power that is incomprehensible to man. Nature feeds our soul's inspiration and so we approach Him through that part of Him which is close to us and within the reach of human understanding. We believe that this great unknown power is everywhere in His creation. The various forms of creation have some of this spirit within them. . . . As every form has some of the intelligent spirit of the Creator, we cannot but reverence all parts of the creation.[1]

The implications of this type of primitive religion are far reaching and have relevance to certain theological and existential problems of historical religions. The problem that particularly concerns us here is the lack today within the historical religions of an adequate metaphysic of nature. Such a metaphysic was certainly present in the origins of the Judeo-Christian tradition, but is now being forgotten. Neglect has left the way open, as we currently have seen in an abundance of tragic examples, for abuses of the natural environment.

Unlike the conceptual categories of Western culture, American Indian traditions generally do not fragment experience into mutually exclusive dichotomies, but tend rather to stress modes of interrelatedness across categories of meaning, never losing sight of an ultimate wholeness. Our animate-inanimate dichotomy, or our categories of animal, vegetable, and mineral, for example, have no meaning for the Indian, who sees that all that exists in animate, each form in its own special way, so that even rocks have a life of their own and are believed to be able to talk under certain conditions. Creatures we relegate to the category "animal" or "bird" and consider inferior to humans, the Indian refers to as "peoples" who, in a sense, have a recognized superiority to humans. It is generally believed that in the order of creation animals were here before humans, and in these cultures what is anterior in time has a certain superiority over that which comes later. (It is this belief that accounts for the enormous respect shown to the aged among Native American peoples.)

This mode of interrelatedness may be seen in the Lakota's discernment of a certain unity underlying that which we perceive generally as very different kinds of beings or phenomena. For example, spiders, elks, bisons, birds, flying insects, and even cottonwood trees have a unifying element, for all these manifest certain relationships to the wind or breath.[2] There is, in fact, a qualitative and comprehensive science of the winds among these peoples that has as its ultimate unifying principle the understanding that as the wind moves or exerts power over the forms of nature and yet in itself is unseen, so it is with the Great Mysterious whose unseen presence gives life and movement to all that is. Such modes of conceptualization are often conveyed through mythical expressions that anthropomorphize the four winds, naming them as brothers identified with the four directions of space, each with his own particular qualities or forces; ultimately the four brothers are seen to be the sons of a single named father figure. There are, of course, other members of this particular family of unlikely associates unified by the wind or breath as principle. Always, however, such configurations are expressed in terms of directly experienced natural phenomena.

The generally understood meaning of the symbol—as a form that stands for or points to, something other than the particular form or expression—is incomprehensible to the Indian. To the Indian's cognitive orientation, meanings generally are intuitively sensed and not secondarily interpreted through analysis; there tends to be a unity between form and idea or content. Here the "symbol" is, in a sense, that to which it refers. The tree at the center of the Sun Dance lodge does not just represent the axis of the world, but *is* that axis and *is* the center of the world. The eagle is not a symbol of the sun, but is the sun in a certain sense; and similarly, the sun is not a symbol of the Creative Principle, but is that Principle as manifested in the sun. When a Navajo singer executes a sand painting of one of the gods, or *Yei*, the painting does not represent the god; the god is really present there and radiates toward all participants at the ceremony its particular grace or power.

It is not that these concepts of the symbol, or of mythic time, are in real contrast to the same concepts of the historical religions. Generally, the contrast is rather between traditional people and modern people who attempt to live in a desacralized world and who govern their lives through the artificial segments of clock-time, through linear rather than circular projections. American Indian traditions speak to us with special force today partly because these traditions, and of course other "exotic" outside traditions, appear to be more total and less hypocritical. They seem to represent a gratifyingly integrated and intense participation across a very wide spectrum of experiences. Aspects of the Indian's world do not become sacralized only within the context of special liturgical occasions (although obviously there are special occasions where intensity is generated), but rather, as is generally the case with peoples close to their primal sources, the total world of experience is seen as being infused with the sacred.

Given the above considerations, it should now be clear that if we are to speak with precision about modes of contemplation and action for American Indians, it will be necessary to examine in detail, and through more specific examples, their modes of understanding their natural environment, and the quality of their structured relationships to specific forms.

With the American Indians we are dealing ultimately with a quality of culture wherein action and contemplation are interrelated and integrated. Or, if we wish to make a sharper distinction between meditation and contemplation, it may be said that special rituals and ceremonials, as well as the routines of everyday life, constitute meditative acts that open, to the exceptional person at least, possibilities for pure contemplation. A hunter, for example, is not just participating in a purely mechanical subsistence activity, but is engaged in a complex of meditative acts, all of which— whether preparatory prayer and purification, pursuit of the quarry, or the sacramental manner by which the animal is slain and subsequently treated—are infused with the sacred. Black Elk described the act of hunting as being—not representing—life's quest for ultimate truth. Hunting is a quest, he insisted, that requires preparatory prayer and sacrifical purification; the diligently followed tracks are signs or intimations of the goal, and final contact or identity with the quarry is the realization of Truth, the ultimate goal of life. Similar examples of hunting as a meditative rite could be presented from the Southwestern peoples, and Frank Speck has found the same attitudes among the Naskapi hunters of the Labrador peninsula.

In their visual art forms, there is no separation between the created form of whatever medium, and the message or power this form bears and transmits. It may be the case that the powers of certain forms must become activated through rite, song, or prayer, yet the power is always latently present in the created design or object. Across the great variety of such created works there cannot, in the first place, be found that occidental distinction between art and craft, for in a primal as in any normal society it would be inconceivable to separate art from life, or the practical from the beautiful.[3]

The natural materials used by the American Indians were always respected in the fullness of their context, that is, as being produced from the sacred substances and generative forces of the earth. "Material" resources were thus gathered with prayer, song, and sacrifice, or even in holy pilgrimage with appropriate formal rites and ceremonies. Every being and natural substance had a life and power of its own that was to be respected, for these powers could be transmitted to humans. The hunting of animals was therefore a ritual activity in which the hunted offered up its being to the hunter. Food and hides and all parts of the animal were therefore understood to partake of this sacrificial act, and of the sacred power of the particular animal. In making objects for special ritual use it was inappropriate even to puncture the hide of the animal with arrow or bullet; certain animals such as the deer or antelope were slain by being run down on foot and then ritually suffocated, so that the sacred life breath of the animal would be contained within its being. If clothing was to be made, care would be taken to honor the animal by not cutting or trimming the hide, but to leave it as if it were still the outer clothing of the being who originally wore it. In wearing such a garment or robe a person would thus partake of the spiritual qualities or powers latent in the particular animal. For in this vision all beings and resources of creation were understood to manifest qualitatively differentiated powers that could be assimilated by man or woman.

All images that were painted or depicted with natural materials were experienced as immediate presences bearing and radiating powers specific to both the form depicted and to the materials used. Quasi-naturalistic representation may have been used for special circumstances, but abstract representation was more prevalent, for in just a single aspect of a depicted being—in the paw of a grizzly bear or in a painted image of an elk track—the full force of the entire being was presented and experienced. In objects of special power, such as the painted hide shields of the Plains Indian, the depicted images were revealed in visions or dreams received through fasting or in retreat, and their protective functions could only become operative through the use of prayer, sacred song, or ritual acts. A style of painting of shamanic origin, diffused across many areas of the Americas, presents animal forms as if they were transparent. Through elegant abstract treatment, the inner vital and generative organs are depicted on the surface of the being, allowing the viewer to penetrate into the most interior and sacred realm. These widespread representations reveal the presiding American Indian vision of creation and process wherein the forms of existence are experienced as the outer shell of interior and spiritual realities.

Stone "effigy" pipes, which are widely diffused in the Americas—and in museums—may be grand examples of aesthetically pleasing and powerful sculpture, but again their full efficacy and power are in the dynamics of their ritual use. When a person smokes, the flow of breath is drawn from the source of life in the central fire-containing bowl, and when the bowl is carved with animal beings facing the one who smokes, a circular relationship, by means of visual image and shared breath, is established. This is typical of almost all American Indian art forms, which express through a multitude of means both relationship and identity. When a vessel is molded from moist clay, relationship with the creative force of the earth is established, the maker becomes Creator, and the completed vessel is a living being, both alive and containing life. This is why the Mimbres painted bowls of Southwest burials are found with holes in the bottom, for in this manner, and appropriate to the occasion, the life of the vessel is ritually killed.

Similar kinds of meditative or contemplative attitudes are present over a vast range of other activities. The southwestern Pima or Papago, or any of the basket-making peoples, perceived in their acts of gathering grasses and vegetable dyes, and in the weaving process itself, the ritual recapitulation of the total process of creation. The completed basket is the universe in an image; and in the manufacturing process the woman actually plays the part of the Creator. Similarly, in establishing the dynamic interrelationship between the vertical warp and the horizontal weft, the Navajo blanket weaver participates in acts that imitate the creation of the universe itself. As indicated above, it may be that the practitioner of such kinds of traditional crafts will not be able to consciously analyze or interpret such "symbolism"; nevertheless, through the force of myth and oral traditions, such values are intuitively sensed and participated in with the total being and not just with the mind.

When a Plains Indian woman decorates a robe with porcupine quills, she is not just involved in making a useful, aesthetically pleasing object. As a member of a women's quillwork "guild" she is obliged to fast and pray before commencing her work, and she must retain a contemplative attitude as she works with the brightly dyed quills. Because of the formal and initiatory nature of the quillworker's guild, the woman will probably be aware of the identity between the porcupine and the sun, and that the sun is a manifestation of the Creative Principle. The quills she lays on in geometrical patterns established by tradition are really rays of the sun and thus eminently sacred. The quillworker has, as it were, trapped the sun, understood as a spiritual principle, upon a garment now of utilitarian, aesthetic, and spiritual value. These values are real and functional both to the maker and to the wearer of the garment. Neither art nor what we call religion are divorced from each other or from life.

Similar modes of spiritual conceptualization are involved in the making of swellings and ceremonial structures: in the tipi, the domed sweat lodge, the Sun Dance lodge of the Plains, the round or octgonal hogan of the Navajo, the wickiup of the Apache, and the long houses of woodland peoples such as the Iroquois or Menomomini. All these dwellings are created in imitation of the process of the creation of the world itself, and are perceived as sacred. They thus serve as supports for meditation. Living with such forms makes it almost impossible to forget the transcendent dimension of life.

A multitude of meditative acts with their supporting forms could be identified across the great diversity of cultures and in relation to a vast range of expressions and activities. A rich array of major rites and ceremonies of special intensity could similarly be presented for many groups, such as the synthetic and profound spiritual meanings expressed in the rites of the sacred pipe; the elaborate four-day communal and sacrificial rites of the Sun Dance of the Plains Indians; the seven- or nine-day Navajo ceremonies for reestablishing the health of a person who has become ill through being in a state of disharmony with the universe; and the complex initiatory rites, such as the *Medewewin*, of many of the woodland peoples. One additional mode of participation in the sacred is the foundation of all that has been presented above, and it brings us perhaps closest to the heart of these cultures. I am referring to the retreat or "vision quest."

Through the vision quest, participated in with physical sacrifice and the utmost humility, the individual is opened in the most direct manner to contact with the spiritual essences underlying the forms of the manifested world. In the states achieved at this level, meditation may be surpassed by contemplation. Thus Black Elk has said that the greatest power in the retreat is contact with silence, "for is not silence the very voice of the Great Spirit?" In certain cultures the retreat is initiatory in character for young men or occasionally for young women, who seek spiritual sanction for a new and sacred name; in the arctic, or among some southwestern peoples, this retreat is participated in only by those who seek the necessary spiritual power for becoming special religious practitioners, a shaman, a medicine man, or a "singer," the term used by the Navajo and the Apache. Among many groups the retreat was specifically associated with the quest for a guardian spirit, although this is not as general a phenomenon as the vision quest itself. Among the Plains people the vision quest was most intensely developed; it was an activity that was expected of every young man, and frequently of every young woman, participated in not just once at a certain time in his or her life, but indeed with frequency throughout the life of the individual. No one in these societies, it was believed, could have success in any of the activities of the culture without the unique spiritual power received through the quest.

The minimal formal elements of the retreat involved the guidance of a spiritual mentor, preliminary rites of purification, the seeking out of an isolated place, usually on a mountain top, and the observance of a total fast. At the place of the retreat, special patterns for the participant's actions, and often special forms of prayer, were indicated to the supplicant by the mentor. Essentially, the person was to be exposed, normally for four days and nights, to the elements and to the forms and forces of nature; he or she should be attentive to whatever might appear, no matter how insignificant the being or phenomenon might seem to be. If a dream should come to the participant while asleep, this too could be of import. Although the dream was considered to be of lesser power, or as auxiliary to the true vision, nevertheless the person should be attentive to such experiences and should be able to relate them to the guide, who might explain their spiritual implications. Indeed, many of Black Elk's dreams seemed to be very close to the vision experience. I recall one such power dream that he recounted to me: "I was taken away from this world into a vast tipi, which seemed to be as large as the world itself, and painted on the inside were every kind of four-legged being, winged being, and all the crawling peoples. These peoples who were there in that lodge, they talked to me, much as I am talking to you."

Not all who sought, or "lamented", for a vision received the experience. When the experience did come, however, it was in the form of some being, a bird or animal, or of the powers and phenomena of the natural world. Usually the being spoke to the supplicant, giving a message revealing some aspect of wisdom which it manifested or possessed. The supplicant, it was believed, thus established an identity, not just with the form in itself, but with the spiritual essence of the form, which conveyed a specific quality of spiritual power. The gradation of such power was recognized in accord with the nature of the experience and the type of being that appeared. Frequently, the animal or bird might become the individual's guardian spirit, which would protect him or her in the events of life; it might instruct in specific virtues, or convey skills and qualities of special importance to the activities of the society. Spiritual powers could be accumulated through the frequency of such vision experiences, and thus always the great leaders of the community were persons who had received powers through many visions. Without the vision a person was considered to be a nobody and could be successful in nothing. Something of this power received by the individual was communicated to the people generally, not only through the special personality of the individual concerned, but the recipient was also required to publicly externalize the experience through a special dance, the sacred songs received, or through the paintings that he or she had made on the shield or garment. Also, to insure the continuing activation of the vision power within the individual, some part of the animal would be worn on his or her person or kept carefully wrapped in a special bundle. Occasionally such bundles could be acquired by others to whom a vision had never come, for it was believed that the spiritual power, once manifested to a particular person, was then operative in and by itself, so long as certain prescribed requirements for the keeping of the bundle were met.

In American Indian cultures the vision experience served in an especially forceful manner to render transparent to the individual some facet of the phenomenal world, revealing aspects of a spiritual world of greater reality underlying this world of appearances. In and through such qualities of experience, consciously or not those barriers are dissolved that have tended to set apart what is experienced as an "outer world"; the vision experience integrates and interrelates these "inner" and "outer" worlds into one. The beings, or whatever might be involved in the vision, serve as intermediaries revealing aspects of reality through which the ultimate reality of the Great Mysterious (Wakan-Tanka) may be contemplated, if not comprehended.

Understood in its total context, this type of religion, with its specific modes of spiritual realization, proceeds in a circular continuum through the domains of action, meditation, and contemplation, leading back again to action. The mysteries of the natural world provide all the spiritual means.

We should understand well that all things are the works of the Great Spirit. We should know that He is within all things: the trees, the grasses, the rivers, the mountains, and the four-legged animals, and the winged peoples; and even more important, we should understand that He is also above all these things and peoples. When we do understand all this deeply in our hearts, then we will fear, and love, and know the Great Spirit, and then we will be and act and live as He intends.[4]

—Black Elk

❖ 6 ❖

The Immediacy
of Mythological
Message

"If we knew and understood fairytales—and by extension the myth—we would not need the scriptures." This insight of profound implication by G. K. Chesterton is indicative of a change from previous centuries when myth was synonymous with fable, fiction, and poetic invention—an account that was interesting and often amusing, but nevertheless always untrue, a connotation that "myth" still conveys in the popular language of today.

Writing of the Huron in the seventh century, Père Raguenau summarizes well the generally accepted and often repeated opinions of that era: "To speak truly, all the nations of those countries have received from their ancestors no knowledge of a God; and, before we set foot here, all that was related about the creation of the world consisted of nothing but myths" (*Relation,* 1647–48).

Due to a growing number of more enlightened and objective contemporary scholars, those of us who live outside of oral mythic traditions have come closer to an understanding of the realities and truths of mythic statements as understood by peoples who still live by their sacred traditions. Such peoples find in their myths, and oral traditions generally, models for human behavior, statements told and ritually enacted that tell of the origins and ultimate realities of existence, accounts and acts that define the sacred and make it immediate in all its mysterious modes of operation. In the spirit of this new understanding the great oriental scholar, Ananda Coomaraswamy, has written:

> The Myth [is] the penultimate truth, of which all experience is the temporal reflection. The mythical narrative is of timeless and placeless validity, true nowever and everywhere. . . . Myth embodies the nearest approach to absolute truth that can be stated in words.[1]

Or elsewhere, "Myth is to history as Universal is to particular."

From this perspective we will examine selected aspects of the mythologies of Native American peoples that relate to what may be called the immediacy of mythological message. There are other possible orientations and uses of the myth, such as the functionalist and structuralist approaches of the contemporary anthropological sciences. These approches often tend to be poverty-stricken exercises, but they may hold value where they serve to clarify and elucidate the sacred dimensions of the mythic statement or accompanying ritual act as understood and lived by the Native American peoples themselves.

There are obviously great diversities in the mythologies held and lived by Native American peoples, and thus in the cosmologies, world views, and religious and ritual expressions, all of which have their origin and reinforcement in the myth. Central to this rich diversity, however, is a common perspective that particularly deserves our attention: a concept of time manifest in all real myths and continually expressed in profound ritual enactments of mythic themes and sacred events—time outside of time, that is, the sacred time of the *hierophany* of the now. The recitation of a myth defining creation, for example, is not experienced in terms of an event of linear time past, but rather of a happening of eternal reality, true and real now and forever, a time on the "knife edge between the past and the future."

To illustrate this immediacy of mythological message as it occurs across the Native Americans' experience, I have selected from an enormous range of possibilities the myths of three groups who are distinct linguistically, culturally, and geographically. The Algonquin "Earth-Diver" myth, because of its profound expression of a form of theism typically and pervasively experienced by many Native American peoples, particularly expresses the perspective of an immediacy of experience. Three interrelated selections from translations of Navajo creation myths express immediacy in other modes, specifically through the perspective of individual identification. Portions of a northern Washington Kathlamet Chinook text, known as "The Sun's Myth," recorded in 1891 by Franz Boas from Charles Cultee, makes a perennial statement concerning the nature of the human soul, of desire and pride, of punishment and subsequent reconciliation, set in the context of the changing events of time. Finally, I wish to stress that the immediacy of the message is conveyed through the use and understanding of language, through the rich and creative variety of means by which myths, and oral traditions generally, are transmitted by the teller.

The "Earth-Diver" myth of the Algonquin peoples of the Eastern Woodlands and the Plains is well known in several of its many versions. The creation of land where there is only water takes place not out of nothingness, but within the perspective of cyclical process, for land was there before this particular deluge, and thus is now underneath the waters and must be recovered. Further, an Earth-Maker figure, Manabush or Nanabozo, the Great Hare among the central Algonquins, or Old Man (*Napi*) among the western Algonquins, is already there upon these waters; in some versions he is holding the peoples' most sacred pipe, often identified with creation and creative power, as among the Algonquin-speaking Arapaho.[2] Indeed, all the aquatic birds and animals are there with Earth Maker, who instructs them to dive down under the waters to find even a small grain of earth from which new land may be made. Typically, the otter, beaver and mink take turns diving under the waters, each being unsuccessful in the mission. After much suspense in the telling of the account, it is always the fourth being, most often the muskrat, who finally surfaces, after four days underwater, with a little bit of earth on his paws.[3] Often this earth is placed upon the back of a turtle, as among the southern Ontario Ojibwa, where the turtle itself represents, or is, the earth as well as fertility. Through the agency of breath Earth Maker then fashions and enlarges the earth, establishing its features and contours until it is again a suitable habitation for all the beings of water and land, finally including human beings.

The key themes in this grand account illustrate a message of immediacy. First, creation here occurs not just once out of nothingness in linear time past, but is an event ever occurring and recurring in cyclical fashion, just as the observable cycle of days or seasons speak of death and rebirth. As with each form of creation, the mystery of this creative cycle of birth, life, death, and life is immediately and continually manifest to one who is attentive. Second, the myth informs us that certain beings, already created, participate and cooperate with the Creator Figure in the act of creation. This again shifts the orientation away from creation understood as a single event of time past, to the reality of those immediately experienced processes of creation ever happening and observable through all the multiple forms and forces of creation.

There are those who might insist that such accounts of a Creator cooperating with creation compromise a more ultimate belief in a Supreme Principle transcendent to all creation. Closer examination of Algonquin beliefs reveals, however, that this is not the case. Among the Blackfeet, for example, it was Old Man (Napi) who requested the animals' cooperation in creating. Napi, however, may refer to many perspectives within creation; he is a trickster and bringer of important cultural forms, and his is also a name for the sun understood in its creative role;[4] but on a more ultimate level, it is believed, this visible sun derives its creative power from an invisible source transcendent to the realm of manifestation and is thus an ultimate Principle. This ultimate Principle is referred to by the Algonquin Ojibwa as Kitchi Manitou, usually translated as Great Spirit, as distinct from manitou, which refers to one of a number of qualitatively differentiated spirit beings or powers. There is a splendid Winnebago account that may serve to clarify this question.

A young man blackened his face and fasted in retreat for four days, for he sought to dream of nothing less than the Earth Maker. "He persevered until he had dreamed of everything in the whole world, but he never saw Ma-o-na," the Earth Maker. Even though the Spirits told him that he *had* dreamed of Ma-o-na because he had dreamed of all his works, the young man still was not satisfied. Finally the youth was given to understand the mystery that Ma-o-na in Himself cannot be seen, and yet at the same time all the visible and experienced forms and forces of creation that the youth had dreamed of are no other than Ma-o-na, so therefore he himself is no other than that.[5]

Formulated in such Native American mythologies are beliefs that serve as a profound and powerful response to the Judeo-Christian form of theism, which tends to insists on monotheism understood in an exclusive sense. Such belief, at least at a certain level of understanding, tends to become excessively remote from the mysteries of observable nature in all her modes of operation. Certainly, students concerned with problems of environmental abuse and degradation have pointed to the ramifications of this possibility. No less than Arnold Toynbee, that great historian of Western religions and civilization, wrote the following in *The New York Times* on September 16, 1973—one of his last pieces of writing before his death.

For premonotheistic man, nature was not just a treasure-trove of "natural resources." Nature was, for him, a goddess, "Mother Earth," and the vegetation that sprang from the earth's surface, the animals that roamed, like man himself, over the earth's surface, and the minerals hiding in the earth's bowels all partook of nature's divinity. The whole of his environment was divine. . . . My observation of the living religion of eastern Asia, and my book knowledge of the extinguished Greek and Roman religion, have made me aware of a startling and disturbing truth: that monotheism, as enunciated in the Book of Genesis, has removed the age-old restraint that was once placed on man's greed by his awe. Man's greedy impulse to exploit nature used to be held in check by his pious worship of nature. This primitive inhibition has been removed by the rise and spread of monotheism.

Native American beliefs in what has been called animism, so indirectly applauded by Toynbee but continually criticized by representatives of the historical monotheistic traditions, need to be understood in the larger contexts, as indicated by the above Algonquin myths, among many others. For neither animism, animatism, nor indeed expressions of polytheism, as they appear in Native American or any legitimate religious traditions, need exclude on other levels underlying concepts of monotheism or beliefs in an ultimate Principle, by whatever name this may be called. If animistic beliefs are understood as being ultimately attached to a unitary Principle, then a way is open to an especially profound realization as the mysteries of creative process, witnessed through every form and force of nature, are immediately experienced in the hierophany of the now.

Native American languages are joined to other sacred languages of the world in the sense that words are not conceived simply as symbols assigned arbitrarily to other units of meaning, as tends to be the case with our own English language. Rather, words in themselves are experienced in an immediate manner as units of power. Thus, to name a being or any element of creation is actually to make manifest the power or quality, soul or spirit, of that which is named. For this reason words and personal sacred names tend to be used carefully in Native American languages; one avoids using one's own or another person's sacred name, and especially, out of both respect and awe, the name of the deceased person. It is due to such a concept of language that N. Scott Momaday has titled his recent autobiography *The Names*; he tells us, "A man's life proceeds from his name, in the way that a river proceeds from its source."[6] He goes on to explain that his identity is achieved through his name which is one point in the river of the generations that preceded him.

Among the Athabaskan Navajo the words of their chantways have compulsive creative power; to name the *yei*, for example—which we inadequately translate as "gods"—is to compel those who are named to be actually, immediately present. Similarly, as the visual counterpart to the audible, the sacred beings of the drypaintings are present in their representations. Sacred curative powers are transmitted through word and form not just to the patient for whom the rites are performed; having been ritually drawn into a center, these powers eventually affect all life as they expand like ripples on the surface of the water when a pebble is dropped.

Against the background of these comments on the language of the Navajo, there follow brief excerpts from four separate Navajo chantway texts involving myths of creation. Although these are separate texts, they interrelate in a cumulative manner.

The first selection is a "sweathouse" song, for among the Navajo, as well as for other Native American peoples, the sweat lodge and its rites are associated with creation.

The earth has been laid down, the earth has been laid down
The earth has been laid down, it has been made.

The earth spirit has been laid down
It is covered over with the growing things, it has
*   been laid down*
The earth has been laid down, it has been made.
The sky has been set up, the sky has been set up
The sky has been set up, it has been made.
The mountains have been laid down, the mountains have
*   been laid down*
The mountains have been laid down, they have been
*   made.*
The mountain spirits have been laid down
They are covered over with all the animals, they have
*   been laid down*
The mountains have been laid down, they have been
*   made.*
The waters have been laid down, the waters have
*   been laid down*
The waters have been laid down, they have been made.
The water spirits have been laid down
They are covered over with the water pollen, they have
*   been laid down*
The waters have been laid down, they have been made.
The clouds have been set up, the clouds have been set up
The clouds have been set up, the clouds have been made.

The establishment of the elements of the earth with their spirit counterparts is recounted here with that creative repetitive rhythmic force typical of Navajo chantways. The following chant extolls the beauty, harmony, and peace of this earth in microcosmic anthromorphic terms.

The Earth is beautiful
The Earth is beautiful
The Earth is beautiful
Below the East, the Earth, its face toward the East, the
*   top of its head is beautiful*

The soles of its feet, they are beautiful
Its legs, they are beautiful
Its body, it is beautiful
Its chest, it is beautiful
Its breath, it is beautiful
Its head-feather, it is beautiful
The Earth is beautiful.

With an earth of beauty created—and also the directions of space extolled in the remainder of the text, which has been omitted here—the following selection describes an ideal interrelationship between the human being and aspects of this created universe.

The Earth is looking at me; she is looking up at me
I am looking down on her
I am happy, she is looking at me
I am happy, I am looking at her.
The Sun is looking at me; he is looking down on me
I am looking up at him
I am happy, he is looking at me
I am happy, I am looking at him.
The Black Sky is looking at me; he is looking down on me
I am looking up at him
I am happy, he is looking at me
I am happy, I am looking at him.
The moon is looking at me; he is looking down on me
I am looking up at him
I am happy, he is looking at me
I am happy, I am looking at him.
The North is looking at me; he is looking across at me
I am looking across at him
I am happy, he is looking at me
I am happy, I am looking at him.

In the final selection, which speaks with special and eloquent force to the perspective of immediacy with which we are particularly concerned, an identity is established between macrocosm and microcosm, between humankind and an earth of beauty, peace, and harmony—qualities expressed in the Navajo word *hozhoni*.

Hozhoni, hozhoni, hozhoni
Hozhoni, hozhoni, hozhoni
The Earth, its life am I, hozhoni, hozhoni
The Earth, its feet are my feet, hozhoni, hozhoni
The Earth, its legs are my legs, hozhoni, hozhoni
The Earth, its body is my body, hozhoni, hozhoni
The Earth, its thoughts are my thoughts, hozhoni,
* hozhoni*
The Earth, its speech is my speech, hozhoni, hozhoni
The Earth, its down-feathers are my down-feathers,
* hozhoni, hozhoni*
The sky, its life am I, hozhoni, hozhoni—
The mountains, their life am I—
Rain-mountain, its life am I—
Changing-Woman, her life am I—
The Sun, its life am I—
Talking God, his life am I—
House God, his life am I—
White corn, its life am I—
Yellow corn, its life am I—
The corn beetle, its life am I—
Hozhoni, hozhoni, hozhoni
Hozhoni, hozhoni, hozhoni[7]

The perspective of immediacy in mythological message is illustrated in the following synopsis of a Kathlamet Chinook text known as the Sun's Myth, which deals with humankind's perennial pride, desire, and subsequent punishment and final reconciliation, a theme not unfamiliar to most of us.

The chief of a village determines to take a journey to find the sun.[8] After using up ten pairs of moccasins and ten pairs of leggings made for him by his wife, he finally arrives at the very large house of the sun. Entering, he meets a prepubescent girl and finds the house filled with painted elkskin blankets, mountain goat blankets, and dressed buckskins decorated with dentalia shells; all the beautiful things prized by these peoples of the Washington coast are itemized in great detail and in repetitive manner. The girl informs the man that these things are being saved for her maturity by her grandmother. Every evening the grandmother returns to the house and hangs up a beautiful object that is shining all over. The village chief finally takes the young girl and is thus offered all the beautiful things hanging in the house. However, he wishes only that one shining object, which the grandmother continually refuses to give to him. Finally he becomes homesick, and, wishing to depart, insists with increasing persistence and anger on taking the shining object with him. The grandmother, after many refusals and warnings, finally hangs the shining object on him, and gives him a stone axe. She tells him to depart and also that she had tried to love him. The text of the myth continues:

He went out,
   Now he went,
      he went home.
         He did not see a land.
            He arrived near his uncle's town.
Now that which he held shook,
   Now that which he held said:
      "We two shall strike your town,
         We two shall strike your town,"
            that which he held said.
His reason became nothing,
   He did it to his uncle's town,

He crushed, crushed, crushed it,
    he killed all the people.
He recovered:
  all those houses are crushed,
    His hands are full of blood.
He thought,
  "O I am a fool!
    See, it is just like that, this thing;
      Why was I made to love it?"
        He tried in vain to wrench it off,
          and his flesh would be pulled.
Now again he went,
  and now he went a little while.
    now again his reason became nothing.
He arrived near another uncle's town.
  Now again it said,
"We two shall strike your town,
We two shall strike your town."
  He tried in vain to still it,
    it was never still.
      He tried in vain to throw it away,
        always his fingers closed.
Now again his reason became nothing,
  now again he did it to his uncle's town,
    he crushed it all.
He recovered:
  his uncle's town [is] nothing;
  all the people have become dead.
Now he cried.
In vain he tried in the fork of a tree,
  there in vain he would try squeezing it off.
    it would not at all come off,
      and his flesh would be pulled.
In vain he would try striking what he held on a stone.
  it would never be crushed.
Again he would go,

he would arrive near another uncle's town.
  now again that which he held would shake:
    "We two shall strike your town,
    We two shall strike your town."
His reason would become nothing,
  he would do it to his uncle's town,
    crush, crush, crush, crush.
      He would destroy all his uncle's town,
        and he would destroy the people.
He would recover,
  he would cry out,
    he would grieve for his relatives.
He would try in vain diving in water,
  he would try in vain to wrench it off,
    and his flesh would be pulled.
      He would try in vain rolling in a thicket,
        he would always try in vain striking what he
        held on a stone.
He would give up.
  Now he would cry out.
Again he would go,
  Now again he would arrive at another town, an uncle's
  town.
    Now again what he held would shake:
      "We two shall strike your town,
      We two shall strike your town."
His reason would become nothing.
  He would do it to the town,
  crush, crush, crush, crush,
    and the people.
He would recover.
  All the people and the town [are] no more.
    His hands and arms [are] only blood.
He would become,
  "Qa! qa! qa! qa!"
  He would cry out.

He would always try in vain striking stones,
  what he held would not be crushed.
    He would always try in vain to throw away what he
    held,
      always his hands enclosed it.
Again he would go,
  Now next [is] his own town,
    he would be near his own town.
      He would try to stand in vain,
        see, his feet would be pulled.
His reason would become nothing,
  he would do it to his town,
  and he would destroy his relatives.
He would recover.
  His town [is] nothing.
    The ground has become full of corpses.
He would become,
  "Qa! qa! qa! qa!"
    he would cry out.
He would try to bathe in vain,
  he would try in vain to wrench off what he wore,
    and his flesh would be pulled.
Some times he would roll about on stones.
  He would think,
    perhaps it will be broken apart.
He would give up.
  Now again he would cry out,
    and he wept.
He looked back,
  now she was standing there, that old woman.
"You,"
  she told him,
    "You.
  I try in vain to love you,
    I try in vain to love your relatives.
Why do you weep?

It is you who choose,
*   now you carried that blanket of mine."*
Now she took it,
*   she took off what he held.*
Now she left him,
*   she went home.*
He stayed there.
*   He went a little distance.*
*   There he built a house, a small house.*[9]

The strength of this account of a perennial condition of the human soul is intensified and made all the more immediate for those who told and heard the myth, for it apparently arose at a time when the traditional values and cultural forms of the people were being lost and destroyed through contact with an alien European culture of conflicting values. Further, the fact that a chief should choose to leave family and village, for whatever purpose, is itself a violation of an ancient prohibition. The theme is thus timeless and universal, but it is also of special import within a particular historical time and for a specific people.

"He built a house, a small house."

The immediacy of the message of mythological statement has been illustrated through three examples of differing perspectives: the polysynthetic theological implications of the Algonquin myth, which speaks of a continuum of experience of the sacred through the manifest forms and forces of a creation ever creating; the perspective of personal wholeness, thus holiness, through identity with an ideal world of beauty, peace, and harmony of the Navajo myth; and finally the powerful Kathlamet Chinook myth relating to a particular time and cultural condition but exposing that universal drama of the human soul—error, punishment-suffering, and final reconciliation. The treatment of these myths, however, remains incomplete without reference to an important dimension of our theme of immediacy: the very medium through which the message is transmitted—the force of oral transmission, what Dennis Tedlock has termed "verbal art."[10]

In addition to the special nature of the Native American languages themselves, as was indicated in the discussion on Navajo chantways, the recounting of the myth is made special through insistence that the telling of the account is serious and potentially dangerous, so that there must be both an appropriate time and place for such telling. Among Native American peoples generally, true myths may be told only after dark and normally in the winter season, after the last thunder of summer and before the first thunder of spring. At this time beings of possible dangerous influence are absent—bears, snakes, and spiders among some peoples. Indeed, severe punishments may occur if this custom is transgressed. The Kiowa believe that if anyone tells a story about their Trickster figure during the day, he will bite their noses off; others believe that one may become a hunchback, or perhaps a snake will come and wrap itself around the teller of the story.

Myths often commence with the phrase, "In the long ago. . . ." This "long ago," it should now be clear, does not refer to a historical period of a linear time past, but usually refers to a qualitative condition of earlier existence which, through the telling of the myth, may be mysteriously reintegrated and realized in the immediacy of the timeless now. Analagous is the "Once upon a time . . ." of European fairytales, which may be translated as "nowever and forever."

A multitude of rhetorical devices are used by the good teller of stories to convey immediacy. He or she may use the first person, and present rather than past tense, thus telling the account as if really present, even actually engaged in dialogue with the figures of the narrative. As a Zuni once told Tedlock, "You're right with that story, like you were in it." Indeed, I still remember vividly the *Iktomi* (Spider) stories old Black Elk liked to tell; you felt that you were right there with Iktomi.

Attention is paid to precise detail, with events in the narrative occurring at specific geographical sites well known in the immediate environment of the listener. Artful utilization of the human voice conveys the sounds of the animals of the narration, and the lengthening of vowels in adjectives and verbs conveys the sense of duration or distance. The intensity of voice is adjusted to fit the particular action being described, or silence may be used to heighten tension or suspense, or may indicate that the narrator is engaged in personal prayer. Skillful manipulation of language and delivery is utilized to fit the character in question. The rich use of metaphor as well as metonymy—where something is named through its distinctive attirbute—serves as a stimulus to the listener's reconstruction of the episode. The beaver, for example, may be referred to among the western Shoshone as "big-tail owner." Ritual enactments often accompany the mythic account, or a multiplicity of props, hand gestures, and mnemonic devices such as the birchbark scrolls of the Ojibwa. Songs specific to a sacred being of the account may be interjected, or even a personal sacred song of the narrator. There are multiple techniques for bringing the audience into the story, and there are careful means for ending the story to insure the constructive and safe return of the listener from mythic time to the present moment through relating and integrating the one into the other. The use of the concluding "that's why" line again contributes to the impact of experiential immediacy. In versions of the Earth-Diver myth, for example—and to return to where we started—Earth Maker holds the muskrat up by his tail in order to take from his webbed feet that soil of which the earth is made, and in so doing stretches out his tail, just as we find it today.

The endings of Native American accounts, whether of

myths or stories, do have moral force, but this is achieved through the use of analogy, or indirectly through the negative activities of the coyote or some trickster figure who engages in all those disreputable things that everyone enjoys hearing of, but always knowing it to be improper conduct. In their great wisdom, Native American accounts, whether of myth or just stories, know where to stop. They never risk alienating their audiences with drawn-out moralizing summaries. In that spirit I shall stretch out no further the muskrat's tail, but shall simply end by saying: "It is so . . ."

Sun Dance: Sacrifice, Renewal, Identity

Where a people's vision speaks of life, sacrificial means for recurrent renewal of all life, and suffering for the identity with the source of life—such vision can neither be destroyed, denied, nor ignored.

The annual Sun Dance ceremonies of the Plains Indians of North America give to these peoples—as indeed to all peoples, today as in the past—a message through example affirming the power of suffering in sacrifice, revealing in rich detail the mystery of the sacred in its operations, in all life, and throughout all creation. Where there is no longer affirmation or means for sacrifice, for "making sacred," where the individual loses the sense of Center, the very energy of the world, it is believed, will run out. Such traditions affirm for those who listen, or indeed inevitably for those who do not, that where the sacred in the world and life is held as irrelevant illusion, where evasion of sacrifice in pursuit of some seeming "good life" becomes a goal unto itself, then in the empty and concomitant ugliness of such a life and human-manipulated world, the ordering cycle of sacrifice will and must be accomplished by nature herself so that again there may be renewal in the world.

In accordance with the mood and perspective of this state-

ment, ethnographic description of the particulars of a Lakota, Arapaho, Gros Ventre, Blackfeet, Cree, Cheyenne, or
Crow/Shoshone Sun Dance is neither appropriate nor necessary. Rather, a composite suggests what is essentially a
single language of sacred act and vision, even though expressed by different groups in multiple rich and varied dialects.

Already in the cold darkness of winter's night there are
preparations in the Plains for spring's advent and that celebration variously called Dance for World and Life Renewal,
Dance Watching the Sun, or the Thirst Dance. Sponsors
come forward, advance vows are made by prospective participants, sacred materials are gathered, songs of power are
learned and transmitted from the old to the young, and
members of these guiding societies meet and prepare for
the "moon of grass growing," the time of spring when the
power of the sun will return to renew the life of the earth, to
bring new strength, goodness, and joy to all of life's beings.
It is the one annual occasion when bands or clans, or even
several allied nations, may come together to celebrate in
solemnity and joy a sacred event, the begining of a new
cycle of life, to insure that the energy of this world and life
will be renewed so that the cycle may continue. For three or
four days of life-shaping formal rites and ceremonies, and in
the additional camp days of preparation and ending, the
individual and group will better know the power of suffering in sacrifice.

To construct from timbers brought from the mountains the
circular ceremonial lodge, the lodge of "new birth," "new
life," the "thirst lodge," is to reenact the creation of world
and cosmos. Horizontally, the lodge doorway situated in
the east is the place whence flows life in light; from the
south comes growth in youth, from the west ripeness, full
fruit, and middle age, and from the north completion and
old age leading to death, which leads again to new life. At
the center of the lodge the most sacred cottonwood tree,

rooted in the womb of mother earth and stretching up and out to the heavens, is the axis of the world and the male generative principle. Into and out of this central point and axis of the lodge flow the powers of the six directions. When men in awful ceremony are actually tied to this Tree of Center with the flesh of their bodies, or when women make offerings of pieces of flesh cut from their arms, sacrifice through suffering is accomplished that the world and all beings may live, that life may be renewed, that human beings may realize their identity.

The qualitative powers of the directions and the effective actualization of sacrifice cannot be operative so long as people retain their impurity. Participants initially purify themselves in the little universe of the round sweat lodge, where purifying forces generously released from the rocks of the earth, from air, fire, and water cleanse them and give new life. Indeed, in the days and nights of ritual ceremony to follow means are used to maintain participants in a state of purity through sacrificial concentration on sun or Center, or through the purifying agency of smoke from tobacco, from burning sweet grass and other wild grasses, or sweet sage and cedar.

Special persons are chosen for specific ritual functions, and they become what they personify: Earth Maker, Lodge Maker, and the venerable sacred woman of purity who is Earth herself in all her powers and with all her blessings. Without the presence of this most sacred woman there can be no Sun Dance, for the duality of cosmic forces, the complementarity of male and female, are essential to the creative act and central to the realization of totality. To better translate cosmic realities and processes into immediate visible and effective experience, the bodies of participants are prayerfully painted with earth colors the forms of sun, moon, stars, hail, lightning, and various elements of nature.

At certain times special altars are constructed upon the earth with simple means but of profound import: a place on the earth is cleared and made sacred, directions of the world are delineated always in reference to the Center; humanity's relationship to the cosmos is established, its true "path of life" defined. Ceremonial pipes, themselves portable altars, are ever present with these earth altars. There is an association between the pipe or the straight pipestem and the central sacred tree, as both are axes, both trace the Way and express the male generative principle, and both speak of sacrifice.

Dancers wear and use whistles made of the wing-bone of an eagle to which eagle plumes are attached. In recreating the cry of the eagle in the powerful rhythm of song, dance, and drum, the eagle is present in voice and being; a human being's vital breath is united with the essence of the sun and life. Through such ritual use of sacred form a human becomes an eagle, and the eagle with its plumes is the sun. At each morning's greeting of the new sun, dancers face the east holding their eagle plumes toward the sun's first rays, bathing the plumes in the new light of life, then placing the plumes in movements of purification of the head and of all parts of the upper body, dancing in the meantime to the rhythm of heroic song. Dignified movements of dance facing the sun of the sacred tree are sustained in the suffering of thirst, day and night through the beat of the drum, the heart and life of the world, now one with humankind's own heart and life. It has often been said that the strength of such identity of rhythm is carried within a person's being many months after the celebrations are completed.

Through rich and varied means specific forms of life are celebrated and honored within the lodge. Decorated trees may be planted, pine trees perhaps for the dancer's arbor; moisture-bearing cattails are offered by friends and relatives for the dancer's bed, or chokecherry bushes are planted in conjunction with sacred rites and altars. High in the fork of the sacred tree there is an offering nest for Thunderbird. Some form or aspect of the bison, and an eagle or a rawhide effigy of a human being, is hung upon the tree. Small children sometimes fashion and bring into the lodge pairs of little clay animals: elks, deer, rabbits, kitfoxes, dogs, otters, even grasshoppers. Thus present within the lodge is that which grows from the earth and those who live in the water, who walk on the earth, and who fly in the air. The powers of all things and all beings are present in the holy place.

The Sun Dance is thus not a celebration by humans for humans; it is an honoring of all life and the source of all life that life may continue, that the circle be a cycle, that all the world and humankind may continue on the path of the cycle of giving, receiving, bearing, being born in suffering, growing, becoming, returning to the earth that which has been given, and finally being born again. Only in sacrifice is sacredness accomplished; only in sacrifice is identity found. It is only through suffering in sacrifice that freedom is finally known and laughter in joy returns to the world.

> *here am I*
> *behold me*
> *I am the sun*
> *behold me*
> —Lakota Sun-Rise Greeting Song

❖ 8 ❖

The Question of "Mysticism"

Contemporary uses of the term "mysticism" and its cognates have come to apply them to a wide variety of often disparate phenomena frequently far removed from the early Christian or original Greek senses of the terms. It may indeed be said that mysticism has become so abused, and levels of reality so confused, that in certain contemporary contexts it may actually express the inverse of, or the grossest parody of, those great mysteries and mystics of the great legitimate and orthodox religious traditions of the world.

Examples of abuse and misuse could be cited from a plethora of modern cults, "the new religions," and popular parodies of legitimate spiritual or mystical ways, not to mention experimentations with instant "mystical experiences" afforded through the agencies of various drugs. To underline certain dimensions of such problems one may recall the statement of Aldous Huxley in *The Doors of Perception,* written in 1954:

> It has always seemed to me possible that, through hypnosis, for example, or auto-hypnosis, by means of systematic meditation, or else by taking the appropriate drug, I might so change my ordinary mode of consciousness as to be able to know, from the inside, what the visionary, the medium, even the mystic were talking about.[1]

That contemporary confusions concerning the prerequisite conditions for true spiritual realization abound is eminently comprehensible and evident to many. Under the forces of a pervasive materialistic outlook spreading essentially from the West and causally related to the erosion of the great spiritual legacies, people have become increasingly prisoners of the limits of their vision and the manner in which they experience their world. In seeking release from this constricting experience of a continually changing physical multiplicity, and motivated by a nostalgia for a lost, more-real world of true freedom, many have turned in every possible direction for alternate answers. However, due to the erosion and spiritual impoverishment of one's own proper tradition, or rather, due to our inability in these times to understanding the true nature of these traditions, there are left no real criteria for discrimination, evaluation, and, eventually, choice rooted in true knowledge. In addition, the quest, often undertaken with the greatest sincerity, may actually be motivated by sentimentality through the self-will of the ego, or the desire—self-defeating in itself—for some otherworldly, liberating mystical experience that nevertheless appears within the realm of limiting phenomena. Under such conditions there is no guarantee that what is found will not lead to further frustration, and often—as is the case with altered states of consciousness through the use of drugs—to sinking within the lower chaotic depth of one's being, and thus to a deepening intensification of the original problem.

One response to this dilemma, already implied above, may perhaps best be phrased through the following question: Is it still possible, given the force of contemporary circumstances, for a person to reestablish his or her broken links with one of the great world religious traditions—that is, with one of those particular and providential expressions of what has been called the *philosophia perennis*, that perennial and timeless wisdom valid "nowever and forever"? That this may be the only way has been affirmed by an

increasing number of scholars of the sacred, such as Ananda
Coomaraswamy, René Guenon, Seyyed Hossein Nasr, and
the great contemporary European theologian and metaphy-
sician Frithjof Schuon, who has unequivocally stated that

> there is no possible spiritual way outside of the great ortho-
> dox traditional ways. A meditation or concentration practised
> at random and outside of tradition will be inoperative, and
> even dangerous in more than one respect; the illusion of
> progress in the absence of real criteria is certainly not the
> least of these dangers.[2]

It has long been necessary to situate correctly the so-
called primitive religions in the context of the world's historical religions, and in so doing to recognize that in spite of
many elements unfamiliar to the outsider, Native American
traditions, at least where there has not been excessive compromise to the modern world, are in no sense inferior, but
indeed are legitimate expressions of the *philosophia perennis*. The injustices suffered by these world views, ritual
practices, and lifeways, through ignorance and ill will,
through deeply rooted prejudices and willful falsifications,
all commencing with the first European contacts with the
New World, now demand that a reevaluation take place and
that proper recognition and respect be given. There are indeed signs today that such positive reassessment is taking
place, and what is especially encouraging is the realization
on the part of many Native Americans themselves who had
lost or neglected their proper religious traditions that such
traditions and related lifeways constitute within the world
of today not only a viable reality in themselves, but also a
valid and powerful response, in terms of fundamental values, to many of the problems faced by the contemporary
world. That there is a progressive strengthening of this realization is nothing short of miraculous when one considers
the pressures for abandoning these traditions, in the name
of "progress" and civilization," that have been exercised
against the people over the past centuries.

One explanation for the current new willingness to understand Native Americans and their lifeways is that, being
rooted in this land for thousands of years, the Indians' other-
wise very diverse cultures have all come to express rich
spiritual relationships with this continent; indeed the forms
and symbols bearing these values are all drawn from the
details of each people's particular geographic environment.
Native Americans lived, and many still do live, what one
might call a metaphysic of nature, spelled out by each group
in great detail, defining responsibilities and the true nature
of that vast web of humankind's cyclical interrelationships
with the elements, the earth, and all that lives upon the
land. The echoes of this message have caught the attention
of at least a few within a society that finally has been forced
by hard circumstances to recognize the gravity of the ecological crisis, and thus to seek answers that speak to root
causes rather than continually treat the ever-recurring
symptoms of the problem.

Many, especially of the younger generations, who for-
merly had turned to distant lands and seemingly exotic traditions for answers to the problems of the world, have now
come to see in expressions of Native American wisdom a
meaningful message, because these sacred traditions are
rooted in and take their expressions from elements of this
very land with which many today, in their alienation, seek
meaningful relationships. Further, many individuals discern a deep mystical element in these sacred traditions of
the Indian, and it is in something of this vision that they
themselves would participate.

However, the problems for the outsider who would per-
sonally relate to the sacred vision and practices of the American Indian are just as critical as, or even more problematic
than, the attempt to relate to any of the orthodox traditions of
East or West. The problem essentially lies in the tendency
for the individual not rooted in any tradition to use an alien
and thus often exotic religious tradition as a screen upon

which to project all that one finds lacking in one's own world. Rarely is the prerequisite effort made to understand the alien tradition on its own terms, through the categories of its proper language, and thus for what it really is in all its profundity and complexity, and with its impelling sacrificial demands. One is too easily satisfied merely to "touch the earth," to nourish one's own personal sentiment and nostalgia, and to hope thereby that somehow a mystic vision of ultimate meaning will automatically and easily come through.

Against the background of the above considerations, it is now possible to ask the following question: If mysticism, in its original and thus deepest sense, is an experiential reality within Native American spiritual traditions, what are the conditions under which such experience becomes operative, and what are some of the contours of its manifestations?

Mysticism, insofar as it is a reality within these native traditions, is not, as the outsider has tended to view it, a vague quality of some supernatural experience that spontaneously comes to individuals whom Providence has allowed to live close to nature. Rather, such mystical experiences are first of all prepared for, and conditioned by, lifelong participation in a particular spoken language that bears sacred power through its vocabulary, structure, and categories of thought, and serves as a vehicle for a large body of orally transmitted traditions, all the themes of which also express elements of the sacred. Secondly, such mystic experiences become more available to those persons who have participated with intensity and sincerity in a large number of exacting rites and ceremonies that have been revealed through time, and that derive ultimately from a transcendent source. There are also, through the nature of the peoples' lifeways rooted in hunting activities, interrelationships informed by the rich oral traditions with all the animal beings and the forms and forces of the natural environment. Further, there is the supporting exposure to a rich heritage of art forms, both visual and audible, many of which are representations of a supernatural experience received by the executor of the form. One may also mention the support offered by the dynamic rhythm of continually living out the myriad details of everyday life, all the forms and acts of which are enriched by the inherent dimensions of the sacred. All these elements and more provide a specific, all-encompassing, supporting frame within which each individual lives out his or her life. Through the conditioning support and force of such spiritual forms and orientations, the individual becomes open to the possibility of receiving in a dream or true vision glimpses of sacred realities borne perhaps by the forms of the natural world, yet more real and permanent than the fleeting relative reality of the immediate world.

Mystical experiences did not come to the people exclusively through the actual vision quest, but also through participation in other rites and ceremonies such as those of purification or the great annual sacrificial Sun Dance, or due simply to the general conditioning powers and sacred content of the totality of their traditions. Good evidence of this is found, for example, in the life of an exceptional man such as Black Elk. His frequent experiences, and the weight of their message and requirements, placed an enormous burden upon him, causing intense suffering throughout his entire life.

Mystical experiences such as the vision, which after all does appear in some phenomenal form, need not be a necessary criterion for, or a proof of, a true and integrated spiritual realization. The experience may simply provide evidence that the recipient has achieved a certain state of realization. Many traditions, it should be recalled, view visions and mystical experiences generally with suspicion, suggesting that they could provide dangerous distractions on the true spiritual way.

What criteria can be used to affirm the spiritual autheniticity of religious traditions such as those of the Native Americans, and the reality of mystical experiences to which such traditions give rise?

The tradition in question must have its origins in a sacred source that is transcendent to the limits of the phenomenal world. All the expressions and extensions of this tradition will then bear the imprint of the sacred, manifested in terms appropriate to the time, place, and condition of humankind. The tradition provides the means, essentially through sacred rites, for contact with and ultimately a return to the transcendent Principle, Origin, or by whatever name this is called. True and integrated progress on such an inner journey demands the means for accomplishing the progressive and accumulative integration of the following elements or spiritual dimensions: (1) purification, understood in a total sense, that is, of body, soul and spirit; (2) spiritual expansion, by which an individual realizes his or her totality and relationship to all that is, and thus integration with, and realization of, the realm of the virtues; (3) identity, or final realization of unity, a state of oneness with the ultimate Principle of all that is. Spiritual expansion is impossible without the prerequisite purification, and ultimate identity is impossible outside the realm of virtue, wholeness, or spiritual expansion. These themes of purification, expansion, and identity are inherent in all the spiritual ways of the orthodox traditions of the world.

In spite of the initial attractiveness of Indian traditions, because they are rooted in this land and because of their seeming "mystical" qualities they are nevertheless generally inaccessible to the non-Native American. However, by taking the pains to learn what one can from Native American traditions one who as yet is unaffiliated with *a* true tradition will be aided in knowing what a tradition is in all its complexity, depth, and richness of cultural expressions. It is then possible to undertake the work of rediscovering the roots of what normally, or historically, should be one's own spiritual heritage, and committing oneself to that heritage with the new vision that distance and perspective often allow. This is a way that demands sacrifice, as do all spiritual ways, but it is not an escape, and it has an integrity and a rigor that must always provide hope.

9

Time and Process

Concepts of time and process are central to the nature of the larger realm of a people's world view. To examine these concepts may be one way to address, and hopefully to clarify, certain dimensions of those current and tragic problems of polarizations across and within the world's populations. Examples of accelerating tensions and violence are all too evident in the contemporary proliferation of ideological revolutions and social, economic, and political disruptions, all more or less interrelated with inevitable energy crises as nations vie for control over the world's material resources so that they may continue to build a world of diminishing returns upon the fragile and illusory foundation of the nonrenewable.

We are all familiar with those self-serving classification systems by which segments of humanity are identified according to First, Second, and Third Worlds, now extended to Fourth and Fifth Worlds due to the increasing complexities of our current global situation. We are also familiar with associated descriptive terms of less formal language: "developing," "emerging," "backward," or "nonliterate", "primitive." It is suspected that our labels and modes of classification do not just describe objective existential situations based on criteria of scientific and technological sophistica-

115

tion, possession and/or access to material natural resources, or quality or type of political system. What is actually projected are idiosyncratic value judgments, not to say latent prejudices, imposed upon world proponents by the First or perhaps Second World populations of such ranking systems.

Imposing value judgments upon others is hardly new to world history; it is indeed most often the material of which history is made. But what is unique today is the scale to which those segments of humanity, whose presiding values are oriented toward unrestrained technological and material advancement, are pressing these values with their concomitant material furniture upon other world populations. The resulting global tensions are multiple, diverse, and complex. But if a comprehensive overview may be risked, there appears to be a polarization between those worlds of scientific/technological sophistication, termed "modern," and those still surviving worlds and miniworlds whose value orientations may be called "traditional." The former tends to be oriented toward the quantitative, secular materiality of this world, and is essentially sustained by concepts of linear time; the latter inclines toward the qualitative, sacred, otherworldly, and spiritual tendencies and qualities that generally are informed and supported by concepts of cyclical time.

If concepts of time and process are central to particular qualities of peoples' world views, and if such views are instrumental in determining or giving definition to a particular quality of life and culture, then at least some clarification of our personal and global tensions may be furthered through better understanding the nature and implications of these contrasting concepts.

Concepts of time that may be termed linear tend to be of relatively recent origin. It emerged with certain Judaic perspectives, became pervasive in the Western world with the beginnings of the European Renaissance, and was intensified through the rapidly changing ideologies of the Reformation. Obviously a concomitant of the progressive detraditionalization of the Western world, this process has proliferated throughout other once traditional worlds with great rapidity. Our current language forms, in association with and supporting a wide range of patterns of behavior, suggest the degree to which such linear perspectives have come to dominate the structure of our everyday thinking, evaluating, and acting.

In terms of process our time is divided into the categories of past, present, and future. Human beings who are oriented toward both past and future are apt to be distracted from the human and spiritual possibilities inherent in the fullness of one's being in the now. Living in the moment of the present allows us to be in immediate and continual interrelationship with the qualities and forces of our natural environment.

Linear time and process is not just a neutral quantitative scale of measurement, but is inseparable from the value orientations that give rise to it in the first place. There is the inevitable assumption that that which came earlier on this scale is somehow inferior to the more recent, or to that in the future toward which we are moving. Idiosyncratic interpretations of Darwinian evolution theories lent support to such assumptions with most gratifying consequences for their adherents, for this new vision sprang from and fed those latent human proclivities, ethno- and egocentricity. Modern people have here found justification for maintaining their assumed inherent, even genetic, superiority over all those other populations of ancient origin who have not yet entered into this new vision of progressive time. Process is now identified with progress, moving onward with ups and downs but inevitably inclining upward.

Such value-laden concepts of time and process completely reversed the traditional cyclical beliefs. They have so permeated our lives and orientations that even certain earlier scholars of the new American anthropological sciences were convinced that the peoples and cultures of their studies, in this case the American Indians, were innately inferior in their humanity and lifeways to people of modern civilization. This belief fed into all those injustices and injuries perpetuated against Native Americans *and* their natural environment, all accomplished under the banner of "manifest destiny," the residues of which still continue to plague us. The Americas have not been the only stages for such tragic play of conflicting values, for such forces have spread to almost all parts of the globe under multiple slogans and justifications through the colonial mentality, through the transference of such a mentality to the new native despots, through prejudices against the grand nomadic traditions. The list goes on.

A core perspective and accompanying human problem, in the concept of linear time and process, is that the line of indefinite extension does not support the situation or experiencing of a center. The linear form suggests, rather, continuity of movement and change from or toward indefinite ends, thus denying the human person the possibility of establishing, of being able to relate to, a true center of permanence that alone can give meaning and direction to change. As has already been mentioned, to forget this truth is to experience a pervasive ever-increasing alienation from nature.

If linear time has thus far been presented as villainous what are the contrasting implications of cyclical time?

With the possible exception of certain Judaic perspectives, the historical religious traditions of the world where they have not been compromised by modernist influences reflect through their rich diversity of means the presiding belief that cyclical, not linear, processes of change are inherent in all of nature in her appearances and modes of operation. Cyclical change, it is further affirmed, can only be possible and meaningful where it proceeds from, and is ever in relation to, the unchanging and immutable, by whatever name this be called. It is all too often forgotten that it is not just the historical religious traditions of the world that have guarded this vision, for this is an understanding that is latent, central, and pervasive to probably all of the so-called primitive or tribal peoples of the world. For these are peoples with traditions of generally more ancient origin than the historical religions, and as such they still guard at least vestiges of primordial traditions.

What are some of the messages that come to us from these traditions? Such peoples celebrate the grand mysteries of the cosmos through seasonal, thus cyclical, rites and ceremonies, supported by rich and varied forms of art, architecture, music, and drama. Through such supporting forms and recreating activities change is recognized and honored, but at the same time it is explicitly affirmed that such change is only possible and meaningful in its relationship to the changeless, which is the center of every circle or cycle.

Such a vision of qualitative process in life and thought is always immediately observable and experienced in all the forms, beings, forces, and changes of the surrounding natural world; and at the center of all change, as at the center of all phenomena, there is recognized the indwelling Presence of ultimate Mystery. Where such quality of belief obtains, it inevitably follows that all the forms and beings of nature are held as sacred and thus treated with respect. As a human being, too, at the center partakes of and is surrounded by this Mystery, he or she is not just a part of creation but is one with the totality of all that is. Where this sense for the sacred is lost there is little else that has the necessary force to control our accelerating waste of resources, unless it is the desperate and ultimate threat, the question of our very survival. For it is always nature who will have the last word.

The rhythm of the cycles of the cosmos, the sun and the seasons, recapitulates the cycle of human life as it moves from birth to death. But where this process, inherent in all nature, is understood in traditional cyclical, not linear manner, death inevitably returns to or joins life so that the cycle may continue. The implications of such beliefs to spiritually meaningful eschatologies are of the greatest importance.

They are important also to a host of gerontological problems. Many years ago, living with a very old Lakota Indian in South Dakota, I observed the manner in which he so closely related to little children. There seemed to be no separation. Asked how he understood the child, he replied, "The child is a person who has just come from the Great Mysterious, and I who am an old man am about to return to the Great Mystery. And so in reality we are very close to each other."

Since many primal peoples live nomadic lives based on hunting animals, the cyclical perspective becomes intensified as human activity is integrated into the cyclical movements, migrations, and life cycles of the animals and birds. Humans assume the sacred responsibility for taking the life of living beings, and so become partners, or links, in the cyclical chain of life and death—that there may be life again. It is for these reasons that hunting is such societies is an eminently sacred activity, providing strong means for the human person to identify existentially with the cyclical modes of nature's operation, and thus with that Center which alone makes the process of the cycle possible.

There is another dimension of particular importance to the quality of life, particularly of the nomadic hunters and gatherers who must live in immediate and continuing contact with animals. In his book *Thinking Animals*, Paul Shepard has detailed how contact with animals is "indispensable to our being human in the fullest sense." He says,

> There is a profound, inescapable need for animals that is in all people everywhere, an urgent requirement for which no substitute exists. It is no vague, romantic, or intangible yearning, no simple sop to our loneliness or nostalgia for Paradise. It is as hard and unavoidable as the compounds of our inner chemistry. It is universal but poorly recognized. It is the peculiar way that animals are used in the growth and development of the human person, in those most priceless qualities which we lump together as "mind."[1]

One of our overriding concerns today is to explore means for achieving principles of unity in the current fragmentation of the sciences. Through dialogue between scientists and humanists or religionists, there lies hope that we may relearn what we have forgotten or denied: namely, that change can have neither meaning nor purpose unless it is in relation to the changeless; that the world of phenomenal appearances has neither reality nor message for the realization of the fullness of our humanity unless it is understood in relation to the Absolute.

10

On Being
Human

O ne component that is frequently and paradoxically lost
sight of is the individual human being; that is, a man
or a woman bearing within himself or herself the totality of
the richness we usually know best in the outer expressions
of those academic disciplines we have come to call by that
useful term, the humanities. The ultimate bearer of culture
is a person who is religiously human within the context of a
traditional heritage.

Many Native American peoples today retain, even though
often in fragmented manner, elements of a heritage of ancient primordial origins. Present within all the dimensions,
forms, and expressions of this heritage, or rather of these
multiple heritages, is a pervasive sense for the sacred. In
one manner or another all life is seen to participate in the
sacred, all cultural forms express the sacred, so that inevitably within this context the lives of those peoples who live
close to their sacred traditions may be called religious, and
they are thus beings who are religiously human. Religion
pervades all of life and life's activities leading a native person once to remark, "We do not believe our religion, we
dance it!"

What then does it mean to be a human person within
these native American cultures? What are the supportive

elements, or traditional means of being and seeing, that contribute to this way of being human in a sacred manner?

Webster's Unabridged Dictionary gives this definition for the word *human*: "Man or his attributes, in distinction from the lower animal world; or, relating to man as distinguished from the superhuman, . . . from the divine . . . , belonging to finite intelligence and power."

On both scores these Western definitions are in direct opposition to the Native American sense of being human. For in the Native American worlds, one does not generally find such quasi-absolute dichotomies between humans and what we call animals, nor on the other hand is humankind by definition considered to be absolutely distinct, separated from divine or sacred power or powers. How then do Native American traditions express such an alternate point of view in their beliefs and lives?

In the multiple expressions of Native American lore, in myths and folktales, in rites, ceremonies, art forms, music, and dances, there is the constant implication of, indeed direct references to, the understanding that animal beings are not lower, that is, inferior to humans, but rather, because they were here first in the order of creation, and with the respect always due to age in these cultures, the animal beings are looked to as guides and teachers of human beings— indeed, in a sense their superiors.

According to a Pawnee account, a great council of all the animals (*Nahurac*) meets in perpetual session in a cave under a round mountain (*Pahok*) (actually located, it is believed, near the Missouri River). These animals monitor the affairs of humans wherever they may be on earth, and if a man or a woman is in need or in trouble and seeks aid in humility, perhaps through the vision quest, the council will choose one of its appropriate members—whether winged, four-legged, or crawling—who will then appear to the man or woman and give something of its own power, or present advice that should thereafter guide the person's life.

Beliefs concerning the nature, authority, and meaning of the animals in these traditions may perhaps be summed up in a general manner. In the people's intense and frequent contact with the powers and qualities of the animals including birds and eventually all forms of life, humankind is awakened to, and thus may realize, all that an individual potentially is as a human person. Human completion, wholeness, or religious awakening depends on this receptive opening up to the potentialities and sacred mysteries in the immediate natural environment. Especially in the nomadic hunting cultures, the oneness of essence underlying the visual differences between humans and animals is stressed; on occasion humans and animals may even be interchangeable.

The theme of reciprocal interrelationship between humans and animals, or more generally between humans and all the forms and forces of nature, is translated onto other levels. There appear specific types of theism, for instance, that contrast markedly with certain quasi-absolute Western dichotomies of human/God, nature/supernatural, matter/spirit. One such example is found in the diverse versions of the widespread Algonquin Earth-Diver myth of creation related previously (p. 85). What is often overlooked, however, is that in diving down through the primordial waters for that little bit of earth, the original aquatic beings were cooperating with First Man, Earth Maker, the All-Spirit, or Maheo, who created four things out of the void: water, light, sky-air, and the peoples of the water, but not yet of the earth. Thus water people were coparticipants in the actual creative process itself. This reinforces respect for the aquatic beings, for the earth and humanity's very being is due to their sacrifice. The myth also suggests that the creative principle itself is not locked into some separate time-space orientation; creation is an eternal, ongoing process of the here and now, in which what is created continues to participate. It is eminently important to this perspective that the account has the water beings say of Maheo, "I know," or, "I see, you must be everywhere."[1]

The full import and impact of oral traditions upon those who live by them, whether myth, folktale, song, or everyday language itself, may only be sensed when the meaning and power of words and names in Native American languages is understood. The majority of Native American names, both personal and sacred, refer to animals, or their qualities, and also to other forms of forces of nature. Further, a person's sacred name, which is never used in everyday speech, was normally obtained through prayer and sacrifice in the vision quest. In everyday Native American languages, words and names have sacred power; one uses them carefully, for their power affects both speaker and hearer.

In his seminal essay "Verbal Art," Dennis Tedlock reminds us that it is the breath that, universally identified with the essence of life itself, and proceeding from the center of a person's being nearest the heart, bears and fashions the word.[2] Interpersonal verbal communication involves the intermingling of the beings' most sacred element, thus establishing through breath made audible the bond of sacred relationship not only between people, but with all phenomena throughout the cosmos.

Not of the order of the myth perhaps, but still critical in the humanizing of individuals at least on the not-unimportant moral or behavioral level, are those rich traditions of tales involving trickster/hero beings and animals—Coyote, Nanabozo the hare, Iktomi the spider. At appropriate times and places the narrator of these tales, through rich and dramatic means, brings to life before the hearer these beings who, in their devious and exciting ventures, define for young and old the perimeters of acceptable behavior. The less-than-human qualities of greed, avarice, selfishness, uncontrolled passions, and sneaky, deceitful, and unaesthetic behavior are graphically and eloquently spelled out. Children and adults get the point and remember in a manner that lecturing and moralizing never accomplish.

As children grow up within the context of their native traditions, they are constantly exposed to forms and actions and ever-widening types of relationships appropriate to the process of becoming a religiously human person. This process commences when the child is in the mother's womb, for especially in this fragile state the being is especially sensitive, it is felt, to all surrounding influences. Barre Toelken tells of a Navajo family close to starvation. The father would not hunt even though there were many deer about, for it was *inappropriate* to take life when a new life was being expected.

The child's first home, the cradle-board of buckskin and specially selected sacred wood (lightning-struck, among the Navajo), provides security and protection for the child not just in its material form but in the sacred powers latent in the wood and the hide, which was once the clothing of the deer itself. A psychological advantage of the cradle-board is that it allows the eyes of the child always to be on the same level as the grown person, the infant never having to look upwards toward the adult. Among the Lakota a young child, especially a girl, is placed in a spider-web type hammock strung out between four trees. In this manner the infant will receive the qualitatively differentiated powers of the four directions of space, and like the spider she may grow up to be an industrious person.

Periods of change or crisis in the life of a boy or girl are recognized as sacred moments of transition. Through rites, ceremonies, and initiations (often traumatic as with the Hopi), the child is enabled to enter into adulthood in a manner that integrates or transforms all that the person had been into what he or she now is. In contrast, Western adults have been taught or forced to eliminate from their being the states of the child, so that too often they live only fragments of what they might and should be.

The so-called arts and crafts of a people, found in such imaginative diversity and aesthetic elegance among Native American peoples, are not just utilitarian, as they are usu-

ally treated by art historians, but represent external projections of a people's inner vision of reality. (The Museum
of Northern Arizona bears above its main portal a statement
to this effect: "Herein Are Exhibited Ideas, Not Things.") It
is through both creating and living with such ideas, values,
sacred powers made tangible, that people are led to realize
who they are in their fullest and deepest potentialities, as
beings religiously human. So it is with the forms and presences of the sacred *Kachina* beings, whether as so-called
dolls, or masked gods, or of the *Yei* who grace the drypaintings with the healing Power of their presence. To wear the
mask is to become that being; to depict the *Yei* is to compel
its sacred presence which is transferred to the patient.

Among the peoples of the Plains there is a tradition of two
types of paintings on bison hides. One style, painted on the
hide of a bison cow and known to art historians as the box
and border design, appropriately may be worn only by
women, for there is depicted on the hide in highly stylized,
abstract manner a kind of vision penetrating into all those
inner vital and generative life forces of the cow, manifesting
all that is most sacred to womanhood. To wear such a robe is
to participate actively in that sacred vision, and thus to be
sacred in the fullness of being human as a woman. As a counterpart, the robe worn by a man is made from the hide of a
bison bull upon which is painted a dynamic solar device,
the sun-burst motif. By wearing such a robe a man participates in the solar power of both the bison bull and the
painted sun, reinforcing the essence of all it is to be a man.
In the shield paintings of the Plains peoples the protective
power is similarly understood to be really present in the
depicted form originally received through a vision experience. As with the power that is one with the spoken audible
word, so also in the visual and dramatic forms of art; the
power of sacredness is really present in the form, whether
painted, quilled, sculptured, or danced.

Traditional Native American ways of seeing and living, of

being human religiously, have things to tell us about ourselves today. Some of the examples may seem remote from the hard problems of contemporary reality for both Native and non-Native Americans. But I am reminded of a statement written by the late John Collier in 1947 (under the chapter heading "The American Indian and the Long Hope").

> They had and have this power for living which our modern world has lost—as world-view and self-view, as tradition and institution, as practical philosophy dominating their societies and as an art supreme among all the arts.
>
> They had what the world has lost. They have it now. What the world has lost, the world must have again, lest it die. Not many years are left to have or have not, to recapture the lost ingredient.[3]

North American Culture Areas

Notes

Chapter 1

1. E. H. Spicer, ed., *Navajo: Perspectives in American Culture Change* (Chicago: University of Chicago Press, 1961), pp. 278–336.

Chapter 2

1. "Chamanism Peau Rouge," *Etudes Traditionnelles* (Paris), November–December 1963.
2. *North American Mythology*, The Mythology of All Races series, Vol. X (Boston, 1916, 1937), p. 77.
3. Black Elk, as told to John G. Neihardt, *Black Elk Speaks* (New York, 1932), pp. 279–280. Reprinted in paperback by the Bison Series of the University of Nebraska Press, 1961.
4. Alice C. Fletcher, *The Hako: A Pawnee Ceremony*, annual report of the Bureau of American Ethnology, XXII, ii, 1904.
5. *Black Elk Speaks*, pp. 198–200.
6. Joseph Epes Brown, *The Sacred Pipe* (Norman, Oklahoma: University of Oklahoma, 1953), pp. xx, 59.
7. *The Sacred Pipe*, p. 115.
8. Melvin R. Gilmore, *Prairie Smoke* (New York: Columbia University Press, 1929), p. 36.
9. *The Sacred Pipe*, pp. 31–32.
10. *The Sacred Pipe*, p. 31.

Chapter 4

1. Frank Waters, "Two Views of Nature: White and Indian," *The South Dakota Review*, May 1964, pp. 28–29.

Chapter 5

1. Carl N. Gorman, "Navajo Vision of Earth and Man," *The Indian Historian*, Winter 1973.

2. Spiders, newly hatched, are carried on long filaments by the winds; the mysterious whistling call of the bull elk, through the use of his breath, attracts the cows to him; a bison cow, breathing over her calf in a cold winter, can enclose the young animal in a protective filmlike sac; birds and insects utilize and exercise control over the winds with their wings; and through the winds a cottonwood tree in season sends out its seeds wrapped in "cotton."

3. One of the great tragedies in the history of world art is that the sacred language of American Indian art forms has been subjected to occidental criteria. Under such impoverished vision museums have tended to exhibit Indian "craft items" as quaint examples of a peoples' "material culture," useful for classifying culture areas, or perhaps for tracing diffusion routes, but never presented as true art. In spite of signs of new awareness on the part of some museum curators and art historians, museums and art books continue to present American Indian arts and crafts as *things,* of aesthetic quality perhaps, but extracted out of the ritual and ceremonial context which is essential to full understanding as this was available to those who created, used, and lived with such forms.

4. *The Sacred Pipe,* p. xx.

Chapter 6

1. Ananda Coomaraswamy, *Hinduism and Buddhism* (Westport, Connecticut: Greenwood Press), p. 6; p. 33, note 21.

2. Cf. John G. Carter, "The Northern Arapaho Flat Pipe," Bureau of American Ethnology, Bulletin 119, 1938.

3. One trait of the muskrat, observed by the people, is to build its house in the water out of mud; the house is dome-shaped and circular as is the earth.

4. George Bird Grinnell, "The Blackfoot Genesis," *Blackfoot Lodge Tales* (Lincoln, Nebraska: University of Nebraska Press, 1962).

5. For the full account see Natalie Curtis, *The Indians' Book* (Harper & Brothers, 1907), pp. 262–263.

6. N. Scott Momaday, *The Names* (New York: Harper & Row, 1976).

7. Recorded by Mary C. Wheelwright, from Hasteen Klah, *Navajo Creation Myth* (Santa Fe, New Mexico: Museum of Navajo Ceremonial Art, 1942; reprinted by AMS, Inc., New York), pp. 136–137, 161, 149, 142.

8. The solar journey, in other myths, may express the opposite of this present version, for a hero may travel to find the sun, or the house of the sun, which is his solar origin. See, for example, *Where the Two Came to Their Father,* Bollingen Series I (Princeton, New Jersey: Princeton University Press, 1969).

9. I have used the unpublished analysis of this Kathlamet Chinook myth as presented by Dell Hymes in his presidential address to the American Folklore Society in November 1974. This myth was originally narrated to Franz Boas in the 1890s by the Kathlamet elder Charles Cultee.

10. In clarifying certain contours of this art I drew heavily on two of Tedlock's seminal article: "Verbal Art" (*Handbook of North American Indians,* vol. 1, chap. 50) and "Towards a Restoration of the Word in the Modern World" (*Alcheringa,* vol. 24, 1976).

Chapter 8
1. Aldous Huxley, *The Doors of Perception* (London: Chatto & Windus, 1954).
2. Frithjof Schuon, "Des Stations de la Sagesse," *France-Asie* (Saigon), 1953, no. 85–86, pp. 507–513.

Chapter 9
1. Paul Shepard, *Thinking Animals* (New York: The Viking Press, 1978), pp. 1–2.

Chapter 10
1. Alice Marriott & Carol K. Rachlin, *American Indian Mythology* (New York: Mentor Books, 1968), p. 39.
2. Dennis Tedlock, "Verbal Art," chapter 50, *Handbook of North American Indians,* vol. 1, ed. by William C. Sturtevant, Smithsonian Institution. Forthcoming.
3. John Collier, *Indians of the Americas* (New York: Mentor Books, 1948), p. 7.